Physical Well-Being Workbook

Facilitator Reproducible Sessions
for Motivated Behavior Modification

John J. Liptak, Ed.D.
Ester R.A. Leutenberg

Duluth, Minnesota

Whole Person
210 West Michigan Street
Duluth, MN 55802-1908

800-247-6789

books@wholeperson.com
www.wholeperson.com

Physical Well-Being Workbook
Facilitator Reproducible Sessions
for Motivated Behavior Modification

Copyright ©2014 by John J. Liptak and Ester R.A. Leutenberg. All rights reserved. Except for short excerpts for review purposes and materials in the assessment, journaling activities, and educational handouts sections, no part of this book may be reproduced or transmitted in any form by any means, electronic or mechanical without permission in writing from the publisher. Self-assessments, exercises, and educational handouts are meant to be photocopied.

All efforts have been made to ensure accuracy of the information contained in this book as of the date published. The author(s) and the publisher expressly disclaim responsibility for any adverse effects arising from the use or application of the information contained herein.

Printed in the United States of America

10 9 8 7 6 5 4 3 2 1

Editorial Director: Carlene Sippola
Art Director: Joy Morgan Dey

Library of Congress Control Number: 2013954177
ISBN: 978-1-57025-307-2

Our thanks to these professionals who make us look good!

Art Director – Joy Dey
Editor and Lifelong Teacher – Eileen Regen
Editorial Director – Carlene Sippola
Proofreader – Jay Leutenberg
Reviewer – Carol Butler

Introduction for the Facilitator

Observable actions and mannerisms that people display when reacting to particular stimuli are called behaviors. Behavior modification involves identifying ineffective behaviors, intentionally targeting them, setting goals for behavioral change, monitoring progress and determining effective rewards for improved behaviors.

The Mind-Body Wellness Series is composed of workbooks designed to help people learn how to discontinue old, destructive health habits and adopt new, healthy lifestyle choices. The model, referred to as Motivated Behavior Modification (MBM), looks at specific learned behaviors and the impact of environmental stimuli on those behaviors. It focuses on helping participants change undesirable and unhealthy lifestyle behaviors by objectively identifying unrealistic behaviors and replacing them with healthier, more effective behaviors.

Physical Well-Being Workbook Sections

Section 1 – Exercise – This chapter will help participants explore how regularly and consistently they engage in exercise and adequate amounts of physical activity in their lives.

Section 2 – Sleep – This chapter will help participants explore the extent to which they are getting both adequate and quality sleep in order to cope with stress and maintain a healthy lifestyle.

Section 3 – Stress – This chapter will help participants determine the various ways that they are able to manage stress in their lives in order to promote physical wellness.

Section 4 – Body Image – This chapter will help participants explore how they feel about their weight and overall body image.

Section 5 – Nutrition – This chapter will help participants explore how well they plan their meals to include nutritional choices and how often they eat nutritiously.

Section 6 – Addiction – This chapter will help participants explore both their propensity to engage in addictive behaviors as well as identify their addictions to substances, activities, and thoughts and behaviors in their lives.

Section 7 – Safety – This chapter helps participants explore their personal level of safety at home, while driving a vehicle, and in their communities.

(Continued on the next page)

Changing Unhealthy Behaviors

Developing healthy lifestyle choices can be difficult, as implied in the adage "It's hard to teach an old dog new tricks!" Developing positive behaviors related to health may be a challenging task for participants, but they can successfully change unhealthy behaviors to healthy ones. MBM (Motivated Behavior Modification) is based on several premises. For participants to be successful, you as the facilitator can enhance their motivation in several ways.

Components of Each Session

1. SELF-ASSESSMENT
Step 1 is the self-assessment of participants' current level of behavior. Encourage participants to take one step at a time. By working on one behavior at a time, the task of changing participants behavior will not feel insurmountable. Because behavior is so difficult to change, it is important that they start with small behaviors and work slowly to change them. By trying to change more than one behavior at a time, people set themselves up for failure. Encourage participants to keep it simple! Each chapter is set up in a step format for MBM.

2. SUPPORT SYSTEM
Step 2 will guide participants to identify their support system for each behavior. Encourage participants to develop a support system to help them change their behavior. It is important that you encourage participants to define who in their lives can help and support them while they are changing their unhealthy behaviors. Encourage them to let people know that they are trying to make genuine behavioral changes and that they don't have to suffer in silence to change an unhealthy behavior to a healthy one. Explain that each participant's support system will vary for each behavior.

3. JOURNALING
Step 3 includes journaling questions to help participants think critically about how they will change their behavior. Encourage participants to write everything down in a journal. Remind them that words are shallow and just saying they are going to make changes will not suffice. They will then engage in self-assessments, work on the exercises in this workbook and write concrete goals.

4. GOAL-SETTING
Step 4 will remind participants not to give up and to be persistent in their efforts. Explain that it takes time to change behaviors and that they should not expect immediate results. The purpose of setting goals is to help each participant take smaller steps leading to the selected overall goal. Encourage them to review and revise their plans for a healthier lifestyle. By developing MBM goals to work toward and achieve, participants will remain motivated while they slowly turn unhealthy habits into healthy ones.

5. MONITORING MY BEHAVIOR
Step 5 will help participants monitor their progress throughout the MBM process. This will assist them to be accountable. If during efforts to make positive changes, participants slip and go back to old behavioral habits, don't let failure stop them. You are their coach and you can encourage them to learn from their failures and use their newfound knowledge to make successful choices.

6. REWARD YOURSELF
Step 6 will ensure that participants reward themselves for each goal success fully achieved. Remind participants to reward themselves when they do make motivated behavioral changes. HEALTHY rewards provide them with positive feedback and further motivate them to continue in their efforts to live a healthier lifestyle.

7. TIPS
Step 7 Participants will benefit from tips on motivational behavior modification which are included as suggestions for processing each session.

(Continued on the next page)

Motivational Barriers to Behavioral Change

Many motivational barriers hinder behavioral change and many of these barriers show up in peoples' thought processes. The impact of thinking on a person's motivation and subsequent behavioral changes can be monumental. Therefore, it is important to watch for any barriers that may be keeping participants from being successful as they work to change their unhealthy behaviors to more healthy ones.

Following are some of the most prominent reasons that bar people from changing their destructive behaviors and implementing a healthy lifestyle program.

- Some people prefer instant gratification and fail to look at the long-term benefits and consequences of their behavior. Even though they know smoking is related to cancer and other diseases they may still smoke for instant gratification.

- Some people continue to engage in unhealthy behaviors, often thinking that they will deal with the consequences at a later date. They may eat junk food, vowing to deal with heart disease at a later date in time. Procrastinators often like the idea of making lifestyle changes, but lack the motivation to begin.

- Some people feel they are too busy to worry about the consequences of unhealthy behaviors. They don't have time to exercise in the morning as they are getting ready for work, and in the evening they are tired from working.

- Some people simply are indifferent to unhealthy behaviors. They will say such things as "Everyone gets sick sometimes" or "We all will die someday!"

- Some people have a sense of invincibility and believe that unhealthy behaviors will not affect them. A habitual alcohol drinker will say such things as "I can drink while I'm young. I'll be sure to quit before it affects my health."

There are probably many more reasons that people resist changing destructive lifestyle habits, but this provides a sampling of the reasons people refuse to implement a healthy lifestyle program.

Oftentimes, people reach mid-life and feel rushed to begin changes in their behaviors, but they are often unable to because the unhealthy lifestyle choices have become habits and sometimes addictions.

Mid-life is often the time when people will "become motivated" and search out specific health-care professionals to "fix" their health-related problems.

(Continued on the next page)

Using this Workbook to Modify Behavior

Behavior Modification programs provide a process to PERMANENTLY change destructive and negative behaviors and replace them with positive behaviors that will lead to greater health and well-being. The behavior modification program included in this series of workbooks contains several critical components:

Motivated Behavior Modification (MBM) Components

STEP 1: Self-Assessment – The first step in modifying behavior involves determining the frequency, circumstances, and outcomes of the behaviors to be altered or enhanced. MBM relies on objective self-assessment to determine each participant's unhealthy lifestyle behaviors and to establish a baseline for their strengths and limitations. Once a baseline is established, the data collected can be used to track a participant's progress in changing unhealthy lifestyle behaviors to more healthy ones. The self-assessments contained in this workbook are referred to as "formative assessments" and can be used to assess participant's current level of functioning and also to measure behavioral change over time.

In this stage, people acknowledge that they have a problem and begin to seriously think about making healthier lifestyle changes. They want to explore in depth the level of their unhealthy lifestyle choices. Self-assessments are very powerful tools for helping participants learn more about themselves to gain valuable insights into their constructive and destructive lifestyle behaviors. Self-assessments are used by participants to better understand themselves and gain valuable insights into their thinking, feelings and behaviors. Self-assessments allow facilitators to gather information about participants to get a complete picture of each person.

Facts about self-assessments:

- Self-assessments provide you with a small sample of behavior and should not be used to stereotype participants. Self-assessments are designed to allow participants to explore their behavioral strengths and weaknesses.

- Factors such as cultural background, handicaps, and age should be taken into consideration when exploring self-assessment results.

- Self-assessments are designed to be self-administered, scored and interpreted by the participants. However, facilitators should be available to assist participants in understanding their scores in an objective and helpful way.

- Self-assessments are designed to gather self-reported data, thus the results are dependent on each participant's motivation and cooperation.

- Self-assessment results should be explored in light of other behavioral data facilitators have available, not in isolation.

- Self-assessments can be used with individual participants or with groups.

- Self-assessments can be used to form specific decisions about the type of instruction that would be most beneficial. Thus, if your group scores lowest on a particular self-assessment for a chapter, that might be an effective place to concentrate instruction.

- Participants can use the results of their self-assessments to adjust and improve their behavior.

(Continued on the next page)

Using this Workbook to Modify Behavior
Motivated Behavior Modification (MBM) Components *(Continued)*

STEP 2: Support System – The next step in behavior modification involves participants recognizing who is in their support system and identifying which people are supportive of which topics. This requires participants to think about who can support them through each particular behavior modification, what their supporters can do, and how they will help. Support people may vary for each behavior. The person who is being supportive about sleep can be different from the one being supportive about an addiction recovery.

STEP 3: Journaling – The next step in behavior modification is journaling answers to specific behavioral questions. Journaling has been shown to be very effective in helping people to think critically about themselves and issues they are coping with. It is wise to remind participants not to concern themselves with grammar or spelling. Just free-writing thoughts and ideas is the purpose of the journal.

STEP 4: Goal Setting – The next step in behavior modification is to set goals to modify behavior. Goals initiate an action plan and are necessary to motivate behavioral change. Participants will set goals that will replace their old, negative habits with new, healthier habits. It is important to help participants determine which specific behaviors they want to change. This will help to give order and context to the change process. Goals provide participants with direction, priorities and a well-conceived action plan for MBM. Goals should meet these criteria:

- **Specific and Behavioral:** Goals must be stated in concrete, behavioral terms. For example, "I would like to lose 10 pounds by summer" would be a concrete, behavioral goal.
- **Measurable:** Goals must be measurable so that people can track their progress. For example, losing weight is too vague to be measured accurately, but losing 10 pounds by summer can be measured.
- **Attainable:** Goals must be within reach or participants will not be motivated to work toward them. They must feel that they have a realistic opportunity to achieve their goals. For example, losing 50 pounds would be very difficult to achieve, thus it would make it unrealistic to maintain motivation.
- **Relevant:** Goals must be important to the participant. For example, knowing that a person who is 10 pounds lighter will be healthier and look better in the summer or perhaps fit into a cherished piece of clothing will help to provide motivation.
- **Time-Specific:** Goals must have specific times for completion if they are going to have power. However, the time frames need to be reasonable and realistic so that participants will feel committed. For example, by setting a goal of losing 10 pounds by summer sets a realistic time frame to accomplish the goal.

The goal setting process helps participants to be personally accountable in changing their unhealthy behaviors.

STEP 5: Monitoring – The next step is to monitor behaviors until desired outcomes are reached. Sections will be included for participants to keep a regular record of their activities and progress. Motivation is the intrinsic drive that pushes participants into action and makes permanent behavioral changes. Motivation is enhanced when participants are working toward specific goals and monitoring their progress as they continue to make motivated behavioral modifications. By monitoring their progress as they move toward goals, participants reinforce MBM.

STEP 6: Rewards – This step defines rewards for accomplishing behavioral goals. Healthy rewards will vary from person to person. Participants will benefit by rewarding themselves for any positive steps taken to change unhealthy behaviors.

STEP 7: Tips – This final step provides insights into ways people can deal with unwanted behaviors.

Introduction for the Participant

Most major health problems today are due to poor lifestyle choices. Many of those choices are learned at an early age and reinforced over time. Your lifestyle choices help to determine who you are now and how healthy you will be in the future. Although many aspects of life are uncontrollable, you do have control over the lifestyle choices you make. You alone can make conscious positive or negative choices that will influence how healthy you are in the future. All your choices, whether large or small, affect your wellness to a degree. Additionally, when you make a choice and then repeat it over time, the impact becomes more effective. For each of the unhealthy choices you have made in the past, you need to find healthy choices you can make now.

Physical wellness is critical in your overall well-being. People who are physically well tend to be physically active and exercise regularly, eat a well-balanced diet, maintain a healthy body weight, get enough sleep, practice safe sex, minimize exposure to unhealthy environmental contaminants, avoid harmful substances, and seek medical attention and advice regularly.

You will discover many benefits from making healthy physical lifestyle choices:

- You will feel healthier and have a better quality of life.
- You will notice quicker recovery from illness, injury and disease.
- You will lower your risk of chronic disease and illness.
- You will be able to deal more effectively with tension and stress.
- You will slow the aging process and extend your longevity.
- You will help to prevent high blood pressure, cholesterol and diabetes.
- You will help to regulate and improve overall bodily functions.
- You will have a healthier mental attitude.

As you can see, you have many reasons to make healthy lifestyle choices and live a healthier life. The biggest challenge is to find ways to take control of your personal health choices and follow a healthy lifestyle.

The purpose of the Physical Well-Being Workbook is to help you make healthy choices and keep you motivated while you modify your behavior. In this workbook, you will engage in various types of self-assessments, you will have an opportunity to set healthy lifestyle goals, and you will focus on living a healthier life.

(Continued on the next page)

Introduction for the Participant *(Continued)*

Some Things to Remember

Developing healthy lifestyle choices can be difficult, as is implied in the adage "It's difficult to teach an old dog new tricks!" Developing positive behaviors related to health can be a challenging task, but successfully changing your behavior can be accomplished.

You can do this!

- Take one step at a time. By working on one behavior at a time, the task of changing your behavior will not feel insurmountable. Because behavior is so difficult to change, it is important to start with small behaviors and work slowly to change one at a time. By trying to change more than one behavior at a time, people set themselves up for failure. Keep it simple!

- Create a support system to help you change your behavior. Who can you ask for help and support in changing your unhealthy behaviors? Choose people with whom you feel comfortable, and people who would be helpful in a specific area of your life who know that you are trying to make changes. You don't have to suffer in silence to successfully change an unhealthy behavior to a healthy one. Let people know about your desire to change and allow others to support you.

- Write everything down on paper. Saying you are going to make changes will not suffice. Self-assessments, working on defined behaviors and writing concrete goals will help you to be successful.

- Be persistent in your effort and do not to give up on yourself. Remember that it takes time to change behaviors. Do not expect immediate results. The purpose of setting goals is to help you take smaller steps leading to your overall goal. Plan for a healthier lifestyle. By developing motivated behavior modification (MBM) goals to work toward and achieve, you will remain motivated while you slowly turn unhealthy habits into healthy ones.

- Be accountable. If during your efforts to make positive changes you slip and go back to old behavioral habits, don't let this stop you. Attempt to learn from your setbacks and use your newfound knowledge to make successful choices. Monitor your progress.

- Reward yourself for a job well done. HEALTHY rewards provide you with positive feedback and motivate you to continue in your efforts to live a healthier lifestyle. You will find ways to reward yourself for a job well done!

- Use the tips, as applicable to you, provided on the last page of each of the sessions.

You are now prepared to begin making motivated behavior modifications (MBMs)! Working through the steps in each section of this workbook will allow you to more easily change unhealthy lifestyle behaviors into more healthy ones. This process really works. It is an exciting way to change your behavior and begin to enjoy and appreciate a happier, healthier life.

Table of Contents

Section I – Exercise
- Step 1: Self-Assessment Introduction and Directions 15
  - Self-Assessment 16
  - Self-Assessment Scoring Directions 17
  - Self-Assessment Profile Interpretation 17
  - Self-Assessment Profile Descriptions 18
- Step 2: Recognize and Develop a Support System 18
- Step 3: Keep a Journal 19
- Step 4: Set Goals 20
- Step 5: Monitor My Behavior – Cardio Vascular Training 21–22
  - Monitor My Behavior – Strength Training 23–24
  - Monitor My Behavior – Flexibility Training 25–26
- Step 6: Reward Myself 27
- Step 7: Tips for Motivated Behavior Modifications 28

Section II – Sleep
- Step 1: Self-Assessment Introduction and Directions 31
  - Self-Assessment 32
  - Self-Assessment Scoring Directions 33
  - Self-Assessment Profile Interpretation 33
  - Self-Assessment Profile Descriptions 34
- Step 2: Recognize and Develop a Support System 34
- Step 3: Keep a Journal 35
  - Journaling – Tracking Your Sleep 36
- Step 4: Set Goals 37
- Step 5: Monitor My Behavior – Environment 38
  - Monitor My Behavior – Eating & Drinking 38
  - Monitor My Behavior – Establish a Sleep Pattern 39
  - Monitor My Behavior – My Bedtime Habits 39
- Step 6: Reward Myself 40
- Step 7: Tips for Motivated Behavior Modifications 41

Section III – Stress
- Step 1: Self-Assessment Introduction and Directions 45
  - Self-Assessment 46
  - Self-Assessment Scoring Directions 47
  - Self-Assessment Profile Interpretation 47
  - Self-Assessment Profile Descriptions 48
- Step 2: Recognize and Develop a Support System 48
- Step 3: Keep a Journal 49
- Step 4: Set Goals 50
- Step 5: Monitor My Behavior – Physical Activity 51–52
  - Monitor My Behavior – Relaxation Techniques 53–54
  - Monitor My Behavior – Time Management 55–56
- Step 6: Reward Myself 57
- Step 7: Tips for Motivated Behavior Modifications 58

Table of Contents

Section IV – Body Image
- Step 1: Self-Assessment Introduction and Directions ... 61
  - Self-Assessment ... 62
  - Self-Assessment Scoring Directions ... 63
  - Self-Assessment Profile Interpretation ... 63
- Step 2: Recognize and Develop a Support System ... 64
- Step 3: Keep a Journal ... 65
- Step 4: Set Goals ... 66
- Step 5: Monitor My Behavior – Food Plan ... 67–68
  - Monitor My Behavior – Exercise ... 69–70
  - Monitor My Behavior – Self-Esteem ... 71–72
- Step 6: Reward Myself ... 73
- Step 7: Tips for Motivated Behavior Modifications ... 74
  - Information about Unhealthy Body Images ... 74

Section V – Nutrition
- Step 1: Self-Assessment Introduction and Directions ... 77
  - Self-Assessment ... 78
  - Self-Assessment Scoring Directions ... 79
  - Self-Assessment Profile Interpretation ... 79
  - Self-Assessment Descriptions ... 80
- Step 2: Recognize and Develop a Support System ... 80
- Step 3: Keep a Journal ... 81
- Step 4: Set Goals ... 82
- Step 5: Monitor My Behavior – Nutritional Habits ... 83–84
- Step 6: Reward Myself ... 85
- Step 7: Tips for Motivated Behavior Modifications ... 86

Section VI – Addiction
- Step 1: Self-Assessment Introduction and Directions ... 89
  - Self-Assessment ... 90
  - Self-Assessment Scoring Directions ... 91
  - Self-Assessment Profile Interpretation ... 91
- Step 2: Recognize and Develop a Support System ... 92
- Step 3: Keep a Journal ... 93
- Step 4: Set Goals ... 94
- Step 5: Monitor My Behavior – Substances ... 95–96
  - Monitor My Behavior – Activities ... 97–98
  - Monitor My Behavior – Thoughts and Behaviors ... 99–100
- Step 6: Reward Myself ... 101
- Step 7: Tips for Motivated Behavior Modifications ... 102

Table of Contents

Section VII – Safety

- Step 1: Self-Assessment Introduction and Directions 105
  - Self-Assessment 106
  - Self-Assessment Scoring Directions 107
  - Self-Assessment Profile Interpretation 107
  - Self-Assessment Descriptions 107
- Step 2: Recognize and Develop a Support System 108
- Step 3: Keep a Journal 109
- Step 4: Set Goals 110
- Step 5: Monitor My Behavior – Home 111–112
  - Monitor My Behavior – Driving 113–114
  - Monitor My Behavior – Community 115–116
- Step 6: Reward Myself 117
- Step 7: Tips for Motivated Behavior Modifications 118

SECTION I

EXERCISE

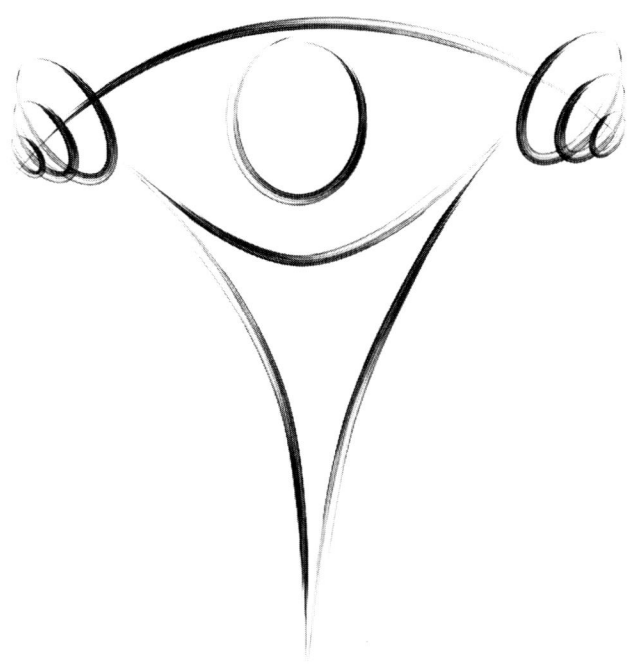

Physical fitness is not only one of the most important keys to a healthy body, it is the basis of dynamic and creative intellectual activity.

— John F. Kennedy

Name _____

Date _____

PHYSICAL WELL-BEING

PHYSICAL WELL-BEING

EXERCISE

Step 1: Self-Assessment Introduction and Directions

Exercise is critical in developing and maintaining your physical health and a sense of wellness. A physically active lifestyle and participation in a lifetime exercise program will contribute measurably to your general health. Although many people engage in physical activities and exercise, they often do not do so regularly and methodically.

The purpose of the Exercise Self-Assessment is to help you explore your general exercise program. Place a check in the boxes that describe your activity and exercise program.

In the following example, the box with a check shows that the person completing the self-assessment rides a bike or stationary bike at least three times a week.

To maintain my physical wellness, at least three times a week . . .

☑ I jog, hike or run

☐ I ride a bike/stationary bike

This is not a test and there are no right or wrong answers. Do not spend too much time thinking about your answers. Your initial response will be the most true for you. Be sure to respond to every statement.

Turn the page and complete the Self-Assessment

PHYSICAL WELL-BEING

EXERCISE

Step 1: Self-Assessment

To maintain my physical wellness, at least three times a week …
- ❑ I jog, hike or run
- ❑ I ride a bike/stationary bike
- ❑ I walk
- ❑ I work in my garden or in my yard
- ❑ I walk instead of riding, whenever it is possible
- ❑ I dance for exercise
- ❑ I play golf or other sports for aerobic exercise
- ❑ I swim or do water aerobics
- ❑ Other_____

CV TOTAL 1_____

To maintain my physical wellness, at least three times a week …
- ❑ I work out with free weights
- ❑ I engage in isometric training
- ❑ I use elastic exercise bands to strengthen my arms
- ❑ I exercise to increase my muscle mass
- ❑ I work out with weight machines
- ❑ I use fixed resistance machines
- ❑ I do push-ups or other strengthening exercises
- ❑ I do pull-ups
- ❑ Other_____

ST TOTAL 2_____

To maintain my physical wellness, at least three times a week …
- ❑ I practice yoga
- ❑ I do stretching exercises
- ❑ I use a partner for stretching
- ❑ I stretch using a chair or a wall
- ❑ I stretch by touching my toes
- ❑ I stretch my back muscles
- ❑ I stretch before more intense exercising
- ❑ I try to stretch each major muscle group
- ❑ Other_____

FT TOTAL 3_____

Go to the Scoring Directions on the next page

PHYSICAL WELL-BEING

EXERCISE

Step 1: Self-Assessment Scoring Directions

Physical activity and exercise can benefit you physically (you will live healthier and longer), psychologically (you will have lower levels of anxiety, less sadness, increased self-esteem, and an enhanced sense of general happiness) and socially (you will have an increased opportunity to meet new people, make new friends and develop new interests).

For each of the sections, count the number of boxes in which you placed a check. You will receive a score from 0 to 9. Put that total on the line marked TOTAL at the end of each section, and then transfer them below. Finally, total the three scores to get your Grand Total (Grand Totals will range from 0 to 27).

CV (Cardiovascular Training)   TOTAL 1   =   _____

ST (Strength Training)   TOTAL 2   =   _____

FT (Flexibility Training)   TOTAL 3   =   _____

                                                      GRAND TOTAL   =   _____

Profile Interpretation

1. If you are participating in one or more of the activities, at least three times a week, listed in each of the categories listed above, you are accomplishing your goal of living a physically-well lifestyle. Keep up the good work, maintain your current level of motivation and consider increasing your activities. The following pages will be helpful to you.

2. If you did not select at least one activity in each of the three categories, it is very important for you to complete the following pages.

3. Next, review the activities listed for each of the three categories (Cardiovascular Training, Strength Training, and Flexibility Training) and identify activities that you would like to try to enhance your physical health and wellness. Place an X after the activities you would like to try. How can you begin participating in those new activities?

Go to the Scale Descriptions on the next page

PHYSICAL WELL-BEING

EXERCISE

Step 1: Self-Assessment Descriptions

Cardiovascular training is intended to enhance your heart's ability to pump oxygen throughout your body. It does this by requiring muscles to perform repetitive behaviors with limited amount of time for rest thus forcing your heart to adapt and increase the amount of oxygen-reinforced blood it pumps to muscles. This type of exercise, referred to as aerobic exercise, is performed in a repetitive manner for a prolonged period of time.

Strength training is intended to increase the sturdiness of your muscles, bones, tendons and ligaments and make your body healthier and less susceptible to injury. Strength training involves keeping targeted muscles activated to near or maximum capacity for short periods of time.

Flexibility training is intended to stretch and manipulate your muscles, tendons, ligaments and joints in order to enhance their range of motion. Flexibility training and/or stretching will work to enhance your body's muscular elasticity and allow your muscles to function more effectively so that you can achieve greater physical performance.

Step 2: Recognize and Develop a Support System

To make the behavioral changes you desire, you need to recognize your current support system and identify who might be helpful to you. Not every supportive person in your life will be helpful for each of your challenges. Complete the following table with people who might be able to support you with your physical activity and exercise behavior.

Supporter	How This Person Can Support Me	How I Can Contact This Person
My friend Jan	Come to the gym with me.	Phone: 000-0000 email: Jan@.com

Keep this list handy. Call, email or text when you need support.

PHYSICAL WELL-BEING

EXERCISE

Step 3: Keep a Journal

The following journaling questions are designed to help you think realistically about the behaviors you want to change.

Remember, your thinking can affect how motivated you are to make healthy changes in your behavior.

What has kept you from participating in more physical activities and exercises?

_____
_____
_____

What excuses do you make to not participate in physical activities and exercise?

_____
_____
_____

In what cardiovascular activities do you intend to increase your participation?

_____
_____
_____

In what strength training activities do you intend to increase your participation?

_____
_____
_____

What flexibility training activities do you intend to increase your participation?

_____
_____
_____

PHYSICAL WELL-BEING

EXERCISE

Step 4: Set Goals

A well-conceived action plan will help you to achieve your goals by keeping you motivated. For your action plan identify both the behavior you want to change and the goals required for you to reach your ultimate physical activity and exercise goals.

The behavior I want to change _____

Goals need to be SMART:
Specific, Measureable, Attainable, Realistic and Time-Specific

Goals	How I will Measure This Goal	How is This Goal Attainable and Realistic?	Time Deadline	How This Will Help Me
I will be more physically active by walking 3 times a week, 6 times around the block.	I will document dates and the number of times I walked around the block.	I can find time every morning before I have breakfast.	2 months	I will have a better attitude because I am doing something for myself to live healthier and longer. I will have more energy.

If you are having trouble identifying goals, consult TIPS, page 28.

PHYSICAL WELL-BEING

EXERCISE

Step 5: Monitor My Behavior – Cardio-Vascular Training

Monitoring your progress toward your goals will help to reinforce your behavior. Keeping track of your behaviors through logs will help you determine what you have accomplished at given times. Periodic re-evaluations support your success. Once you reach your goal(s), set new ones to improve or maintain what you have already achieved. Use a separate page for each change.

EXAMPLE:

My healthy behavior change _Walk more._

My goal _Walk 3 times a week, 6 times around the block._

Date	My Accomplishment	How It Felt
1/1/2014	I walked once around the block.	I was very tired but felt good about myself.

Cardio-Vascular Training

My healthy behavior change

My goal _____

Date	My Accomplishment	How It Felt

(Continued on the next page)

PHYSICAL WELL-BEING

EXERCISE

Step 5: Monitor My Behavior
Cardio-Vascular Training *(Continued)*

How can you increase your cardio-vascular exercising?

_____
_____
_____
_____
_____

What obstacles do you anticipate?

_____
_____
_____
_____
_____

How can you overcome those obstacles?

_____
_____
_____
_____
_____

How will your efforts to increase your cardio-vascular health help you?

_____
_____
_____
_____
_____

PHYSICAL WELL-BEING

EXERCISE

Step 5: Monitor My Behavior – Strength Training

Monitoring your progress toward your goals will help to reinforce your behavior. Keeping track of your behaviors through logs will help you determine what you have accomplished at given times. Periodic re-evaluations support your success. Once you reach your goal(s), set new ones to improve or maintain what you have already achieved. Use a separate page for each change.

EXAMPLE:
My healthy behavior change Start doing push-ups.

My goal Do 2 sets of 10 push-ups every day.

Date	My Accomplishment	How It Felt
1/1/2014	I did 1 set of 5 push ups today.	I wasn't too tired but didn't want to overdo. I felt good.

Strength Training

My healthy behavior change _____

My goal _____

Date	My Accomplishment	How It Felt

(Continued on the next page)

PHYSICAL WELL-BEING

EXERCISE

Step 5: Monitor My Behavior
Strength Training *(Continued)*

What do you like about strength training?

_____
_____
_____
_____

What is difficult about strength training?

_____
_____
_____
_____

What obstacles do you anticipate?

_____
_____
_____
_____

How can you overcome those obstacles?

_____
_____
_____
_____

PHYSICAL WELL-BEING

PHYSICAL WELL-BEING

EXERCISE

Step 5: Monitor My Behavior – Flexibility Training

Monitoring your progress toward your goals will help to reinforce your behavior. Keeping track of your behaviors through logs will help you determine what you have accomplished at given times. Periodic re-evaluations support your success. Once you reach your goal(s), set new ones to improve or maintain what you have already achieved. Use a separate page for each change.

EXAMPLE:

My healthy behavior change   Take up Yoga.

My goal   Take classes and then be able to practice three days a week for at least 45 minutes.

Date	My Accomplishment	How It Felt
1/1/2014	I took my first class.	I liked it more than I thought I would!

Flexibility Training

My healthy behavior change _____

My goal _____

Date	My Accomplishment	How It Felt

(Continued on the next page)

PHYSICAL WELL-BEING

EXERCISE

Step 5: Monitor My Behavior
Flexibility Training *(Continued)*

Which flexibility training have you tried before? How long did you do it?

_____
_____
_____
_____

What obstacles do you anticipate?

_____
_____
_____
_____

How can you get past those obstacles?

_____
_____
_____
_____

In what ways are you hoping flexibility training will help you physically? Mentally?

_____
_____
_____
_____

PHYSICAL WELL-BEING

EXERCISE

Step 6: Reward Myself

People who reward themselves are more likely to continue to exercise than people who don't! The challenge is to decide what reward would motivate you to reach an exercise goal.

Your reward needs to be something that will give you the incentive to achieve your goals. It needs to be healthy, within your budget and something you'll be excited about. If you are buying yourself something, be sure your reward is something you wouldn't ordinarily buy or do. Brainstorm some possible rewards.

- Rewards that would be meaningful to me _____
- Small rewards I could give myself _____
- Large rewards I could give myself _____
- Things that would not cost money and would be fun _____
- Rewards that I can afford and that would be fun _____
- Rewards that I enjoy alone _____
- Rewards I enjoy with people who support me _____

You deserve a pat on the back for the hard work you are completing in this chapter. Rewards help you to pay attention to your triumphs, not your setbacks. Rewards will create good feelings and propel you to want to work harder to reach your goals. Whenever you have completed or achieved one of your goals, treat yourself to one of the items on your list. You can also reward yourself by giving yourself positive affirmations when you have achieved a goal. Below are some samples. Cut them out and post in visible spots at home and work! If these don't work for your goal, write your own on sticky notes!

I exercised today!	Good for me!	I knew that once I got started, I could do it!
I feel so good!	I felt energized after exercising!	I am proud of ME!
I felt good all day after exercising.	I found the time to exercise!	I was a more pleasant person all day!

Aside from the rewards you give to yourself, you will have given yourself at least seven benefits of regular physical activity, according to the Mayo Clinic: weight control, lowered risk of diseases, improved moods, energy boosts, better sleep, more of a spark in your sex life and the fun of physical activity.

© 2014 WHOLE PERSON ASSOCIATES, 210 WEST MICHIGAN ST., DULUTH MN 55802-1908 ▪ 800-247-6789

EXERCISE

Step 7: Tips For Motivated Behavior Modifications

Cardiovascular Training

- Set aside a regular time for exercise and give your workout sessions priority in your weekly plans.

- When you begin to feel too tired or unmotivated to engage in exercises, call, email or text people in your support system to keep you going.

- Cardiovascular training can take a variety of forms including swimming, running, walking, jogging, working out in a gym, riding a bicycle and engaging in aerobic exercises.

- Begin cardiovascular training by taking the stairs instead of escalators and elevators, walking to the store rather than riding, parking the car far away from the door, and joining a gym rather than going shopping or surfing the Internet.

Strength Training

- You can develop a strength training program with or without weights. Choose the option that meets your physical wellness objectives.

- Change your appearance by adding muscles and reducing the size of your fat deposits.

- A program of using a moderate number of lifting repetitions and weight will improve your physical fitness.

- Abdominal crunches (sit-ups) are helpful in flattening your abdomen.

Flexibility Training

- Much of flexibility training is primarily designed to increase your range of motion and alleviate or prevent back and neck pains and strains.

- Stretch your back and hamstring muscles at least three times per week.

- Physical arts like tai chi and yoga, blend physical wellness and spirituality, and can be very effective in promoting mobility and flexibility.

- As a warm up, stretch your neck, back, shoulders, hamstrings, calves and Achilles tendons before exercising.

SECTION II

SLEEP

*For many people, sleep is disrupted because of
the anxieties they have taken to bed with them.
This is where meditation can help . . .
Don't watch the nightly news just before bed,
and don't check your computer
to see where warfare is breaking out.
Do whatever it takes to put yourself at peace.*

— **Gene Bammel, PhD**

Name _____

Date _____

PHYSICAL WELL-BEING

PHYSICAL WELL-BEING

SLEEP

Step 1: Self-Assessment Introduction and Directions

Sleep is essential in coping with stress and maintaining your physical health and sense of wellness. With sufficient sleep, you are able to face challenges effectively and cope with daily frustrations and hassles.

The purpose of the Sleep Self-Assessment is to help you explore the effectiveness of your sleep patterns. Read each of the statements and decide how much the statement describes you. For each of the statements listed, circle the word TRUE if the statement is true for you, and false if the statement is FALSE for you.

In the following example, the circled TRUE indicates the person completing the self-assessment is unable to control the temperature in the room when sleeping.

My sleep environment makes sleeping difficult because . . .

I am unable to control the room temperature in my bedroom . . . . (TRUE)   FALSE

This is not a test and there are no right or wrong answers. Do not spend too much time thinking about your answers. Your initial response will be the most true for you. Be sure to respond to every statement.

Turn the page and complete the Self-Assessment

PHYSICAL WELL-BEING

SLEEP

Step 1: Self-Assessment

My sleep environment makes sleeping difficult because . . .

I am unable to control the room temperature in my bedroom	TRUE	FALSE
I snore or someone I sleep with snores	TRUE	FALSE
I have a computer, books, iPad, iPod or television in my bedroom	TRUE	FALSE
I have bright lights shining through my windows	TRUE	FALSE
I have noisy neighbors / roommates / family	TRUE	FALSE
I can hear outside noise	TRUE	FALSE
I have an uncomfortable mattress or hard to adjust pillow	TRUE	FALSE

ENV TOTAL _____

Before bed . . .

I drink alcoholic beverages	TRUE	FALSE
I use nicotine	TRUE	FALSE
I drink caffeinated coffee, tea or soda	TRUE	FALSE
I eat chocolate	TRUE	FALSE
I use over-the-counter medicines that interferes with my sleep	TRUE	FALSE
I eat "junk" foods	TRUE	FALSE
I overeat	TRUE	FALSE

EAT TOTAL _____

Before bed . . .

I exercise	TRUE	FALSE
I work too much	TRUE	FALSE
I take several naps during the day and/or early evening	TRUE	FALSE
I balance my checkbook	TRUE	FALSE
I get into heated debates	TRUE	FALSE
I work on the computer too long	TRUE	FALSE
I think about the next day	TRUE	FALSE

ACT TOTAL _____

During bedtime . . .

I sleepwalk and/or talk	TRUE	FALSE
I don't have continuous sleep	TRUE	FALSE
I have to go to the bathroom often	TRUE	FALSE
I go to sleep and get up at different times each day	TRUE	FALSE
I don't get adequate sleep	TRUE	FALSE
I feel stressed	TRUE	FALSE
I am in discomfort or pain	TRUE	FALSE

HAB TOTAL _____

(Go to the Scoring Directions on the next page)

PHYSICAL WELL-BEING

SLEEP

Step 1: Self-Assessment Scoring Directions

Falling asleep and staying asleep may sound easy, but for some people getting enough sleep, and getting good quality sleep, is difficult. Sleep is critical to your ability to function effectively.

For each of the four sections on the previous pages, total the false responses you circled. Put that total on the line marked TOTAL at the end of each section. Then, transfer your totals to the spaces below:

ENV (Environment) TOTAL = _____

EAT (Eating) TOTAL = _____

ACT (Actions) TOTAL = _____

HAB (Habits) TOTAL = _____

GRAND TOTAL = _____

Profile Interpretation

Total Individual Scores	Grand Total Score	Result	Indications
Scores from 6 to 7	Scores from 20 to 28	High	If you scored in this range on any of the self-assessments, most or all of your sleep habits are healthy.
Scores from 4 to 5	Scores from 15 - 19	Moderate	If you scored in this range on any of the self-assessments, you have developed some sleep habits that are keeping you from a good night's sleep and living a healthy lifestyle.
Scores from 0 to 3	Scores from 0 to 14	Low	If you scored in this range on any of the self-assessments, you have developed many sleep habits that are keeping you from a good night's sleep and living a healthy lifestyle.

For self-assessments in which you scored in the **Moderate** or **Low** range, find the descriptions on the pages that follow. Then, read the description and complete the exercises that are included. No matter how you scored, low, moderate or high, you will benefit from **every one of these exercises**.

PHYSICAL WELL-BEING

SLEEP

Step 1: Self-Assessment Descriptions

ENV (Environment) – People scoring low on this self-assessment are unable to sleep due to their allowing distractions that keep them from being able to sleep.

EAT (Eating) – People scoring low on this self-assessment are unable to sleep because they have unhealthy eating and drinking habits before bedtime.

ACT (Actions) – People scoring low on this self-assessment engage in activities before bedtime that keep them from being able to sleep.

HAB (Habits) – People scoring low on this self-assessment have ineffective sleep habits or sleeping conditions.

Step 2: Recognize and Develop a Support System

To be able to make the behavioral changes you desire, you need to recognize your current support system and identify who might be helpful to you. Not every supportive person in your life will be helpful for each of your challenges. Complete the following table with people who might be able to support you with your sleep behavior modification.

Supporter	How This Person Can Support Me	How I Can Contact This Person
My Aunt Lucy	By checking on me to be sure I set my alarm and go to bed at the same time each evening.	Phone only, 097-6543

Keep this list handy. Call, email or text when you need support.

PHYSICAL WELL-BEING

SLEEP

Step 3: Keep a Journal

The following journaling exercises are designed to help you think thoroughly about the behaviors related to sleep that you need to change. Remember, your thinking can affect how motivated you are to make healthy changes in your behavior.

How much sleep is enough for you?_____

How often do you get that much sleep? _____

If not very often, why not? _____
_____

How does that amount of sleep allow you to wake up on time and be alert all day? Explain. _____
_____

If you take a nap, how long is the nap? _____ When do you take it?_____

How do you feel when you do not get enough sleep during the night?
_____

What is your going to sleep schedule and waking up schedule?_____
_____

If you do not have a schedule, why not? _____
_____

How can you create a schedule?_____
_____

Have you checked with your doctor to find out if your OTC medications or prescriptions interfere with sleep? _____ If you haven't checked, now is the time.

How dark and comfortable is your bedroom? What can you do to make it more comfortable?
_____
_____

What have you tried before bedtime? A warm bath, yoga, progressive muscle relaxation, guided imagery CDs?
_____

What other things have you tried?_____
_____
_____

© 2014 WHOLE PERSON ASSOCIATES, 210 WEST MICHIGAN ST., DULUTH MN 55802-1908 • 800-247-6789

PHYSICAL WELL-BEING

SLEEP

Step 3: Keep a Journal – Track My Sleep

It is important to keep track of your sleep rituals over time. Using this page, for one week, journal about the time you go to bed, the time you awaken, the number of hours you sleep, how you feel when you awaken, and anything else you want to journal about.

Day	Bedtime	Ritual	Wake up Time	How I Slept	How I Felt Upon Wakening and Other Notes
Sun.					
Mon.					
Tues.					
Wed.					
Thurs.					
Fri.					
Sat.					

How are your bedtime rituals related to how you feel?

_____

_____

_____

PHYSICAL WELL-BEING

SLEEP

Step 4: Set Goals

A well-conceived action plan will help you to achieve your goals by keeping you motivated. For your action plan, identify both the behavior you want to change and specific goals, or smaller goals required to reach your ultimate sleep goals.

The sleep behavior I want to change is _____

Goals need to be SMART:
Specific, Measureable, Attainable, Realistic and Time-Specific

Goals	How I Will Measure This Goal	How is This Goal Attainable and Realistic?	Time Deadline	How This Will Help Me
EXAMPLE: I will not have coffee after dinner	I will have coffee at dinner time and that's it!	Yes, I can do it. I'll drink water after dinner.	I will try for one week.	Hopefully I will get a better night's sleep.

If you are having trouble identifying goals, consult the TIPS, page 41.

PHYSICAL WELL-BEING

SLEEP

Step 5: Monitor My Behavior

Monitoring your progress toward your goals will help to reinforce your behavior. Keeping track of your behaviors through logs will help you determine what you have accomplished at given times. Periodic re-evaluations support your success. Once you reach your goal(s), set new ones to improve or maintain what you have already achieved. Use a separate page for each change.

Environment

The environment in which you sleep must be conducive to relaxation and promote healthy sleep patterns. Record some of the reasons you cannot sleep in your current bedroom.

Why I Can't Sleep	The Cause	How I Can Change the Environment

Eating & Drinking Habits

What are some of the eating and sleeping habits you have before going to bed?

Foods	How Much I Eat and Drink	How Food Keeps Me Awake

(Continued on the next page)

PHYSICAL WELL-BEING

SLEEP

Step 5: Monitor My Behavior *(Continued)*

Establish a Sleep Pattern

Before you go to bed, what do you typically do up to thirty minutes before falling asleep?

What I Do	How Much	How It Makes Me Feel	What Might be Better

My Bedtime Habits

What are some of your bedtime habits?

My Bedtime Habits	How This Habit Affects Me in a Positive or Negative Way	If It Is a Negative Way, How Can I Change This?

PHYSICAL WELL-BEING

SLEEP

Step 6: Reward Myself

People who reward themselves are more likely to achieve adequate sleep than people who don't! The challenge is to decide what reward would motivate you to reach a sleep goal.

Your reward needs to be something that will give you the incentive to achieve your goals. It needs to be within your budget and something you'll be excited about. If you are buying yourself something, be sure your reward is something you wouldn't ordinarily buy or do.

Brainstorm some possible rewards.

- Rewards that would be meaningful to me _____
- Small rewards I could give myself _____
- Large rewards I could give myself _____
- Things that would not cost money and that would be fun _____
- Rewards I can afford that would be fun _____
- Rewards that I can enjoy alone _____
- Rewards I can enjoy with people who support you _____

You deserve a pat on the back for the hard work you are completing in this chapter. Rewards help you to pay attention to your triumphs, not your setbacks. Rewards will create good feelings and propel you to want to work harder to reach your goals. Whenever you have completed or achieved one of your goals, treat yourself to one of the items on your list.

You can also reward yourself by giving yourself positive affirmations when you have achieved a goal. Below are some samples. Cut them out and post in visible spots at home and work! If these don't work for your goal, write your own on sticky notes!

Yes! I had a good night's sleep!	Good for me!	I knew I could do it!
I am so happy for me!	I feel so much better after sleeping well!	I deserve a gold star!
I feel well-rested today.	I have so much energy after a good night's sleep!	I'm not as disagreeable when I sleep well!

A ruffled mind makes a restless pillow. — **Charlotte Brontë**

PHYSICAL WELL-BEING

SLEEP

Step 7: Tips for Motivated Behavior Modification

- Regular exercise early in the day can help you to sleep more deeply. Exercise allows you to release emotional and physical tension that can keep you from sleeping well. Through exercise, you will be more relaxed and able to sleep. However, exercise before bed can leave your body in an aroused state which make sleep harder to achieve.

- Establish a regular, consistent sleep routine. Try to go to bed at the same time each night and wake up the same time each morning to establish a routine.

- Establish a consistent pre-bedtime routine: read a book, solve crossword puzzles. Avoid any activities that might induce stress such as checking e-mails or working.

- Relaxation techniques can be helpful in inducing sleep. Four relaxation techniques you can try are meditation, visual imagery, muscle tension and then relaxing meditative exercises.

- Avoid stimulants that can keep you awake: nicotine, caffeine, energy drinks, sodas and chocolate.

- If napping during the day decreases your ability to sleep at night, then you need to substitute another relaxing activity for your rest time.

- Try to minimize the noise in your bedroom. Avoid having the television or radio playing when you are trying to sleep. If there is too much noise, you can always wear ear plugs to bed.

- Be careful of what you eat and drink immediately before bedtime. Drinking alcohol or high caffeine beverages, and/or eating large amounts of food can hinder your ability to fall asleep and stay asleep.

- If you absolutely can't get to sleep - it may be best to simply get out of bed and read, write a list of topics on your mind, watch television (but not the nightly news!) - anything that will occupy your mind and relax you. When you are feeling drowsy, go back to bed.

- If your mind is "racing" from negative thoughts about the events of your life, you need to find a way to turn off these thoughts. Several methods you can try to stop your negative stream of thoughts include staying in the present and not thinking about events in the future, meditating by counting your breaths, simply saying "Stop!" or write them down, fold the paper and put it into a specially designated box.

- Try taking a warm bath (or some relaxing activity) before bed.

- Repeating comforting phrases or affirmations may help.

PHYSICAL WELL-BEING

SECTION III
STRESS

*How we perceive a situation and how
we react to it is the basis of our stress.
If you focus on the negative in any situation,
you can expect high stress levels.
However, if you try and see the good
in the situation, your stress levels
will greatly diminish.*

– **Catherine Pulsifer**

Name _____

Date _____

PHYSICAL WELL-BEING

STRESS

Step 1: Self-Assessment Introduction and Directions

Stress is a burst of energy telling our body what to do. Eustress is another name for good stress, the helpful type of stress. It is the stress that can help you accomplish good things in your life, and it can be a factor motivating us to move forward, enjoy events and accomplish actions that require some effort but provide satisfaction. Eustress can help you accomplish tasks, goals, and projects. The secret, however, is to plan for this good stress, and to learn to change from experiencing distress to eustress. Eustress becomes distress when it becomes overpowering.

Even though stress may not always be comfortable for you, it is not always a bad thing if you experience it in moderate amounts and you maintain control over your responses. In fact, stress can be very beneficial in helping you deal with challenges and difficult situations. While too much stress can be destructive, a little bit of stress can stimulate you to be prepared, work harder and perform your best. The secret is to view challenges as opportunities, maintain a positive attitude, try to control only what you can, and plan for success.

Anyone attempting to be successful today will certainly encounter eustress and distress in their work and their life in general. Because society and the world have become so unpredictable, working under pressure seems almost inevitable. Although you probably accept stress as a normal part of your everyday life, you still need to find ways to cope with it and use it to your advantage.

This section can help you identify and explore how well you cope with stress as part of your overall physical wellness plan.

This self-assessment contains 21 statements related to your physical stress management habits. Read each of the statements and decide whether or not the statement describes you. If the statement does describe you, circle the number in the YES column. If the statement does not describe you, circle the number in the NO column.

In the following example, the circled number under YES indicates the statement is descriptive of the person completing the inventory.

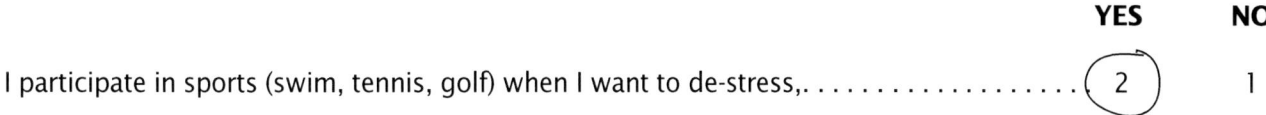

This is not a test and there are no right or wrong answers. Do not spend too much time thinking about your answers. Your initial response will be the most true for you. Be sure to respond to every statement.

Turn the page and complete the Self-Assessment

PHYSICAL WELL-BEING

STRESS

Step 1: Self-Assessment

| | YES | NO |

I participate sports (swim, tennis, golf) when I want to de-stress 2   1

I engage in physical activities to help me de-stress. 2   1

I exercise when I feel frustrated. 2   1

I do aerobic exercises when I start to feel stressed 2   1

I walk, jog, or run to lower my stress-level 2   1

I work around the house to relieve anger and stress. 2   1

Any physical activity makes me feel better 2   1

PA – TOTAL _____

I stretch or do yoga to de-stress 2   1

I take time for hobbies and fun activities 2   1

I take time for simple pleasures. 2   1

I meditate often to remain calmer 2   1

I am able to relax when I feel stressed 2   1

I use relaxation techniques 2   1

I tense my muscles and then relax them. 2   1

RT – TOTAL _____

I use a daily planner. 2   1

I delegate activities that others can do 2   1

I plan ahead for distractions 2   1

I prioritize my tasks and then do the most timely one 2   1

I select one task, concentrate on it and see it through 2   1

I am able to eliminate distractions to get tasks done 2   1

I set goals, prioritize them and work toward them 2   1

TM – TOTAL _____

(Go to the Scoring Directions on the next page)

PHYSICAL WELL-BEING

STRESS

Step 1: Self-Assessment Scoring Directions

The Stress Self-Assessment is designed to help you identify the ways that you manage stress. On the self-assessment page, add the numbers that you circled in each section and write the scores on each of the TOTAL lines. You will receive a total in the range from 7 to 14. Then, transfer those numbers to the spaces below.

> PA   **Physical Activity**   Total   =   _____
>
> RT   **Relaxation Techniques**   Total   =   _____
>
> TM   **Time Management**   Total   =   _____
>
> Now add the three scores together for a **Grand Total** = _____

Profile Interpretation

Individual Score	Grand Total Score	Result	Indications
7 to 9	21 to 27	Low	If you scored in this range on any of the self-assessments, or the total of all of them, a few of your stress habits are healthy. You need to develop many more healthy habits.
10 to 11	28 to 35	Moderate	If you scored in this range on any of the self-assessments, or the total of all of them, some of your stress habits are healthy. You need to develop more healthy habits.
12 to 14	36 to 42	High	If you scored in this range on any of the self-assessments, or the total of all of them, a most of your stress habits are healthy. Continue to develop even more healthy habits.

No matter how you scored on the Stress Self-Assessment (Low, Moderate or High), you will benefit from doing all of the following exercises.

PHYSICAL WELL-BEING

STRESS

Step 1: Self-Assessment Descriptions

Physical Activity is critical in coping with stress. People scoring high on this self-assessment are able to combat the effects of stress by engaging in activities that decrease tension. Some of these activities might include sports such as golfing, swimming, tennis, softball, volleyball; exercising such as doing aerobics, weight training, martial arts, running, and walking; or working in and around the house.

Relaxation Techniques help people to overcome stress by relaxing the body. People scoring high on this self-assessment are able to cope with stress through such techniques as progressive muscle relaxation, deep breathing exercises, visual imagery, mediation, and ability to identify tense body parts that need relaxation.

Time Management skills will help you to feel less rushed. People scoring high on this self-assessment are able to manage their time so that it does not manage them. They are able to pace themselves and effectively manage the demands on their time. They set goals, complete one task at a time, and prioritize their work.

Step 2: Recognize and Develop a Support System

To make the behavioral changes you desire, you need to recognize your current support system and identify who might be helpful to you. Not every supportive person in your life will be helpful for each of your challenges. Complete the following table with people who might be able to support you with your stress control behaviors.

Supporter	How This Person Can Support Me	How I Can Contact This Person
My friend Grace	By reading a guided imagery exercise to me that I found online.	phone or text: 000-0001 email: grace22@.com.

Keep this list handy. Call, email or text when you need support.

PHYSICAL WELL-BEING

STRESS

Step 3: Keep a Journal

The following journaling questions are designed to help you think with a sharp eye and open mind about the behaviors you want to change. Remember, your thinking can affect how motivated you are to make healthy changes in your behavior.

What or who are the major sources of stress in your life now?

___

Describe what you view as a stress-free life for yourself.

___

How are your stressors currently affecting you?

___

How does your body react to stress (get angry, face gets red, hard to breathe, etc.)?

___

What stress-management techniques are you currently using?

___

PHYSICAL WELL-BEING

STRESS

Step 4: Set Goals

A well-conceived action plan will help you to achieve your goals by keeping you motivated. For your action plan, identify both the behavior you want to change and specific goals, or smaller goals required to reach your ultimate stress management goals.

The behavior I want to change is _____

Goals need to be SMART:
Specific, Measureable, Attainable, Realistic and Time-Specific

Goals	How I Will Measure This Goal	How is This Goal Attainable and Realistic?	Time Deadline	How This Will Help Me
Walking more	I will measure one mile and walk it four days per week.	Yes, if I'm not able I can reduce to one-half mile.	Starting this week, I will continure through the summer.	I will expend some energy and probably find creative solutions to my stressors.

If you are having trouble identifying goals, consult the TIPS, page 58.

PHYSICAL WELL-BEING

STRESS

Step 5: Monitor My Behavior – Physical Activity

Monitoring your progress toward your goals will help to reinforce your behavior. Keeping track of your behaviors through logs will help you determine where you are at given times. Periodic re-evaluations are vital for your success. Once you reach your goal(s), set new ones to improve or maintain what you have already achieved. Use a separate page for each change.

EXAMPLE:

My healthy behavior change Go to the gym.

My goal Exercise 3–4 times a week for an hour.

Date	My Accomplishment	How It Felt
1/1/2014	I went to the gym, stayed 20 minutes.	I was a little sore, but I'm going back in 2 days.

✂ -

Physical Activity

My healthy behavior change _____

My goal _____

Date	My Accomplishment	How It Felt

(Continued on the next page)

PHYSICAL WELL-BEING

STRESS

Step 5: Monitor My Behavior
Physical Activity (Continued)

What do you like about physical activities in general? Explain.

_____
_____
_____
_____

What do you dislike about physical activities in general? Explain.

_____
_____
_____
_____

How are you getting your physical activity now?

_____
_____
_____
_____

What obstacles do you anticipate in reaching your goal(s)?

_____
_____
_____
_____

What gain do you anticipate when reaching your goal(s)?

_____
_____
_____
_____

PHYSICAL WELL-BEING

STRESS

Step 5: Monitor My Behavior – Relaxation Techniques

Monitoring your progress toward your goals will help to reinforce your behavior. Keeping track of your behaviors through logs will help you determine what you have accomplished at given times. Periodic re-evaluations promote your success. Once you reach your goal(s), set new ones to improve or maintain what you have already achieved. Use a separate page for each change.

EXAMPLE:

My healthy behavior change Begin playing chess again.

My goal Find a chess club that I like within the next two weeks.

Date	My Accomplishment	How It Felt
1/1/2014	I called several people who are in chess clubs.	Felt good once I decided to visit several this week.

-- --

Relaxation Techniques

My healthy behavior change _____

My goal _____

Date	My Accomplishment	How It Felt

(Continued on the next page)

PHYSICAL WELL-BEING

STRESS

Step 5: Monitor My Behavior
Relaxation Techniques *(Continued)*

When, or in what situations, do you find it difficult to relax?

___

Why is it so difficult for you to relax?

___

What seems to help you relax?

___

What activities do you participate in that you find yourself more relaxed?

___

How can you incorporate more of these activities in your everyday life?

___

PHYSICAL WELL-BEING

STRESS

Step 5: Monitor My Behavior – Time Management

EXAMPLE:

My healthy behavior change Stop my multi-tasking.

My goal Prioritize tasks on a "Things-To-Do" list and do one at a time.

Date	My Accomplishment	How It Felt
1/1/2014	I completed the top 3 tasks on my list.	I felt satisfied when I did one thing at a time and then checked it off my list.

✂ -

Time Management

My healthy behavior change _____

My goal _____

Date	My Accomplishment	How It Felt

(Continued on the next page)

© 2014 WHOLE PERSON ASSOCIATES, 210 WEST MICHIGAN ST., DULUTH MN 55802-1908 ▪ 800-247-6789

PHYSICAL WELL-BEING

STRESS

Step 5: Monitor My Behavior
Time Management *(Continued)*

What are your consistent time management issues? (home, work, family, etc.)

_____
_____
_____

How are you affected by your time management issues?

_____
_____
_____

How are others in your life affected by your time management issues?

_____
_____
_____

What is going to be difficult about adopting new time-management behaviors?

_____
_____
_____

What will you gain by adopting new time-management behaviors?

_____
_____
_____

PHYSICAL WELL-BEING

STRESS

Step 6: Reward Myself

People who reward themselves are more likely to continue to reduce their stress than people who don't! The challenge is to decide what reward would motivate you to reach a stress-management goal. Your reward needs to be something that will give you the incentive to achieve your goals. It needs to be within your budget and something you'll be excited about. If you are buying yourself something, be sure your reward is something you wouldn't ordinarily buy or do.

Brainstorm possible rewards.
- Rewards that would be meaningful to me _____
- Small rewards I provide for myself _____
- Large rewards I provide for myself _____
- Things that would not cost money and would be fun _____
- Rewards that I can afford and that would be fun _____
- Rewards that I can enjoy alone _____
- Rewards I can enjoy with people who support you _____

You deserve a pat on the back for the hard work you are completing in this section. Rewards help you to pay attention to you triumphs, not your setbacks. Rewards will create good feelings and propel you to want to work harder to reach your goals. Whenever you have completed or achieved one of your goals, treat yourself to one of the items on your list.

You can also reward yourself by giving yourself positive affirmations when achieving a goal. Cut them out and post in visible spots everywhere! If these don't work for your goal, write your own on sticky notes!

Yes! I was able to manage my stress today!	Good for me – I feel better!	I feel accomplished when I manage my stress better.
Deep breathing helped!	I am so proud of myself for being on time all day!	I'm not as cranky when I am not stressed.
I am doing OK!	I feel so much calmer after exercising!	It felt good to be prompt!

Although the great feelings you get from stress management can be their own reward, in starting any new habit, it helps to also have some more tangible rewards.... The rewards you give yourself are a personal choice, and you probably know what would be the best incentive for your own success, but I recommend something small and enjoyable.

— **Elizabeth Scott, M.S.**

PHYSICAL WELL-BEING

STRESS

Step 7: Tips for Motivated Behavior Modification

Physical Activity

- Increasing involvement in various types of sports can help you to manage stress. Whether you participate in sports through a formal club (organized tennis club) or with members of your family or friends, physical activity will increase your ability to manage stress.

- Exercising is an excellent way to engage in physical activity. Aerobic exercises, running, jogging, and walking all aid in releasing endorphins that help reduce stress.

- Working around your house (indoors or outdoors) can be an excellent way to de-stress.

- Establish a regular routine for activities you intend to do. For example, if you plan to walk, establish a pattern in which you walk three nights a week for a mile after work.

Relaxation Techniques

- Try engaging in a service-learning project. Many people find that by helping others through volunteering, they are able to feel good about themselves, help others, and relieve stress at the same time.

- Try learning meditation, progressive muscle relaxation, or visualization techniques to help you relax before, during, or after a stressful day.

- Recreational time is not wasted time. Continue to engage in fun, relaxing activities that will help you to maintain your physical wellness.

Time Management

- Using a daily planner to organize yourself will help you remember important names and appointments and simplify your day. Your notes will help to keep you organized and prevent you from wasting time.

- Delegate tasks that someone else can do for you.

- Learn to say "no" to activities that keep you from getting important tasks done. You are only one person and can do only so much. Being assertive and telling others "no" will keep you from overloading your daily schedule.

- Eliminate distractions. If possible, either remove the distractions or temporarily remove yourself from them. This way you can spend more uninterrupted quality time completing your tasks.

SECTION IV

BODY IMAGE

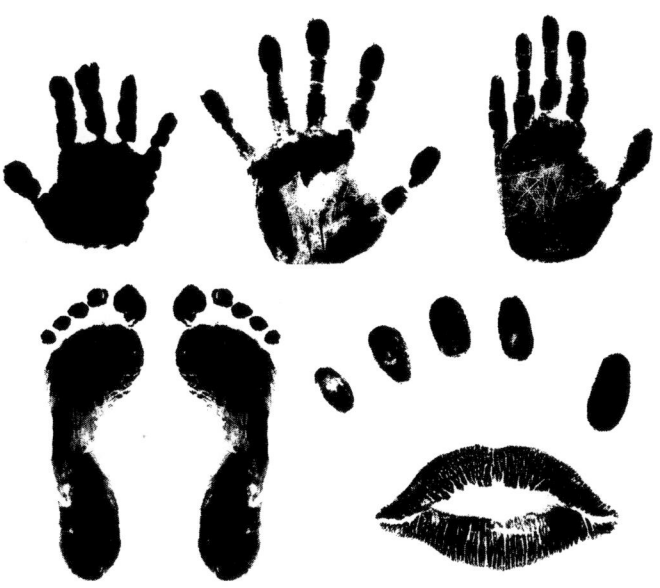

*There is nothing more rare, nor more beautiful,
than a woman being unapologetically herself;
comfortable in her perfect imperfection.
To me, that is the true essence of beauty.*

— **Steve Maraboli**

Name _____

Date _____

PHYSICAL WELL-BEING

PHYSICAL WELL-BEING

BODY IMAGE

Step 1: Self-Assessment Introduction and Directions

Your body image is the picture you have of yourself inside your head. People with a good body image tend to be more confident, self-assured and assertive. When people are dissatisfied with their body image or are unrealistic as to what their body actually looks like, these negative self images affect their physical wellness.

This self-assessment contains 20 statements related to how you view your body. Read each of the statements and decide whether or not the statement describes you. If the statement describes you, circle the number under the YES column, next to that item. If the statement does not describe you, circle the number under the NO column, next to that item.

In the following example, the circled number under YES indicates the statement is descriptive of the person completing the inventory.

	YES	NO
I do not like to look at my body in mirrors	(1)	2

This is not a test and there are no right or wrong answers. Do not spend too much time thinking about your answers. Your initial response will be the most true for you. Be sure to respond to every statement.

Turn the page and complete the Self-Assessment

PHYSICAL WELL-BEING

BODY IMAGE

Step 1: Self-Assessment

	YES	NO
I do not like to look at my body in mirrors	1	2
I am good looking	2	1
I am constantly on a diet or weight loss program	1	2
I think my body is ugly	1	2
I'm embarrassed about my body	1	2
I don't do certain activities because of my appearance	1	2
I am ashamed to be seen in public	1	2
I believe that others think my body is attractive	2	1
I think people are embarrassed to be seen with me	1	2
I am not self-conscious about my weight	2	1
The appearance of my body preoccupies my thinking	1	2
I am not self-critical about my appearance	2	1
My thoughts about my body are negative	1	2
I cannot enjoy activities because I am worried about my body	1	2
I don't go out with friends/family because of my appearance	1	2
I rarely compare my appearance to that of others	2	1
I like to see others who are heavier than me	1	2
I am unhappy with my weight but others tell me I look fine	1	2
I don't try to live up to the "ideal" appearance of the popular culture	2	1
I want to look like a model	1	2

TOTAL = _____

Go to the Scoring Directions on the next page

BODY IMAGE

Step 1: Self-Assessment Scoring Directions

Body Image is the mental image that you have of your physical appearance. This mental image includes how much you weigh, your image of the perfect body, how your weight is distributed, how you compare yourself to people around you and people you see on television and in movies, and your concept of your optimal appearance. Your body image is primarily influenced by three factors:

- Your food plan
- Your amount of exercise
- Your self-esteem about your body

For the self-assessment you just completed, add the numbers that you circled. Transfer the total to the space below.

Body Image Total   =   _____

Profile Interpretation

Total Score	Result	Indications
20 to 32	Low	If you scored in this range on any of the self-assessments, your body image is not very healthy. You need to develop a healthy attitude about your body image with healthy habits.
33 to 36	Moderate	If you scored in this range on any of the self-assessments, your body image is somewhat healthy. You need to continue to develop a healthy attitude about your body image with healthy habits.
37 to 40	High	If you scored in this range on any of the self-assessments, your body image is healthy. Continue developing a healthy attitude about your body image with healthy habits.

No matter how you scored (Low, Moderate or High) you will benefit from doing all of the following exercises.

PHYSICAL WELL-BEING

BODY IMAGE

Step 2: Recognize and Develop a Support System

Your body image is critical to your physical health; therefore, the following table will help you to stabilize your body image. To be able to make the behavioral changes you desire, you need to recognize your current support system and identify others who might be helpful to you. Complete the following table with people who might be in your support system.

Supporter	How This Person Can Support Me	How I Can Contact This Person
My Mom	By reminding me in her gentle way of what I already know.	phone: 000-000-0000

Keep this list handy. Call, email or text when you need support.

PHYSICAL WELL-BEING

BODY IMAGE

Step 3: Keep a Journal

The following journaling questions are designed to help you think carefully about the behaviors you want to change. Please remember that your thinking can affect how motivated you are to make healthy changes in your behavior.

In what ways are you satisfied with your body?
_____
_____
_____

How would you like to change your body?
_____
_____
_____

Do others close to you believe you need to change your body? Explain.
_____
_____
_____

How will changing your body enhance how you feel about yourself?
_____
_____
_____

What is the source of dissatisfaction with your body (from you? your family members? your friends?)
_____
_____
_____

What do you think your perfect body looks like?
_____
_____
_____

PHYSICAL WELL-BEING

BODY IMAGE

Step 4: Set Goals

A well-conceived action plan will help you to achieve your body-image goals by keeping you motivated. For your action plan, identify both the behavior you want to change and specific goals, or smaller goals required to reach your ultimate body image goals.

The behavior I want to change is _____

Goals need to be SMART:
Specific, Measureable, Attainable, Realistic and Time-Specific

Goals	How I Will Measure Each Goal	How is Each Goal Attainable and Realistic?	Time Deadline	How This Change Will Help Me
I want to be more satisfied with my body.	My weight – I want to lose 10 pounds.	I need to choose my food and drinks properly and begin exercising.	My daughter's graduation.	I will feel more comfortable when I go out in public.

If you are having trouble identifying goals, consult the TIPS, page 74.

PHYSICAL WELL-BEING

BODY IMAGE

Step 5: Monitor My Behavior – My Food Plan

Monitoring your progress toward your goals will help to reinforce your behavior. Keeping track of your behaviors through logs will help you determine what you have accomplished at given times. Periodic re-evaluations are vital for your success. Once you reach your goal(s), set new ones to improve or maintain what you have already achieved. Use a separate page for each change.

EXAMPLE:

My healthy behavior change Eat more fruits and vegetables.

My goal At my next physical checkup in 3 months record lower cholesterol and weight levels.

Date	My Accomplishment	How It Felt
1/1/2014	I went to the gym, stayed 20 minutes.	I was a little sore, but I'm going back in 2 days.

✂ -

Food Plan

My healthy behavior change _____

My goal _____

Date	My Accomplishment	How It Felt

(Continued on the next page)

PHYSICAL WELL-BEING

BODY IMAGE

Step 5: Monitor My Behavior
Food Plan (Continued)

For you, what is difficult about following a healthy food plan?
_____
_____
_____

How can you begin to reduce the portions you eat?
_____
_____
_____

What foods or drinks do you need to eliminate from your daily life?
_____
_____
_____

What foods or drinks can you add to your regular daily life.
_____
_____
_____

How can you eat differently at others' homes or restaurants?
_____
_____
_____

How can you maintain healthy eating habits over time?
_____
_____
_____

PHYSICAL WELL-BEING

BODY IMAGE

Step 5: Monitor My Behavior – Exercise

Monitoring your progress toward your goals will help to reinforce your behavior. Keeping track of your behaviors through logs will help you determine what you have accomplished at given times. Periodic re-evaluations promote your success. Once you reach your goal(s), set new ones to improve or maintain what you have already achieved. Use a separate page for each change.

EXAMPLE:
My healthy behavior change Walk outdoors or in the mall.

My goal Every single day I want to walk a mile.

Date	My Accomplishment	How It Felt
1/1/2014	I went to the mall and walked a quarter of a mile.	Satisfying! Better than I thought it would.

✂ —

Exercise

My healthy behavior change _____

My goal _____

Date	My Accomplishment	How It Felt

(Continued on the next page)

PHYSICAL WELL-BEING

BODY IMAGE

Step 5: Monitor My Behavior – Exercise *(Continued)*

In the past, has exercise been appealing or unappealing to you? Explain.

_____
_____
_____

If exercise is appealing, what obstacles get in your way now?

_____
_____
_____

If exercise is appealing, what can you do to make it more appealing?

_____
_____
_____

Would you rather exercise with someone or by yourself?

_____
_____
_____

If you prefer exercising with someone, with whom can you pair up?

_____
_____
_____

If you prefer exercising alone, what can you do to enjoy it more?

_____
_____
_____

PHYSICAL WELL-BEING

BODY IMAGE

Step 5: Monitor My Behavior – Self-Esteem

Monitoring your progress toward your goals will help to reinforce your behavior. Keeping track of your behaviors through logs will help you determine what you have accomplished at given times. Periodic re-evaluations promote your success. Once you reach your goal(s), set new ones to improve or maintain what you have already achieved. Use a separate page for each change.

EXAMPLE:
My healthy behavior change   To be helpful for my body.

My goal   To make two or more positive statements about my body daily.

Date	My Accomplishment	How It Felt
1/1/2014	I made one positive statement about my body.	Difficult, but I'll aim for two tomorrow.

- -

Self-Esteem

My healthy behavior change _____

My goal _____

Date	My Accomplishment	How It Felt

(Continued on the next page)

PHYSICAL WELL-BEING

BODY IMAGE

Step 5: Monitor My Behavior – Self-Esteem (Continued)

How can you begin to feel better about your body, and ultimately, yourself?
___
___
___

What negative thoughts keep popping into your head about your body?
___
___
___

What can you say to yourself when you have those negative thoughts?
___
___
___

What can you do, in healthy ways, to like your body more?
___
___
___

Who in your life boosts your self-esteem and helps you to feel good about yourself?
___
___
___

How can you spend more time with those people? (Be sure to help them to feel good about themselves, too!)
___
___
___

PHYSICAL WELL-BEING

BODY IMAGE

Step 6: Reward Myself

People who reward themselves are more likely to continue to improve their body image than people who don't! The challenge is to decide what reward would motivate you to reach a goal you have set. Your reward needs to be something that will give you the incentive to achieve your goals. It needs to be within your budget and something you'll be excited about. If you are buying yourself something, be sure your reward is something you wouldn't ordinarily buy or do.

Brainstorm possible rewards.
- Rewards that would be meaningful to me _____
- Small rewards I provide for myself _____
- Large rewards I provide for myself _____
- Things that would not cost money and would be fun _____
- Rewards that I can afford and that would be fun _____
- Rewards that I can enjoy alone _____
- Rewards I can enjoy with people who support you _____

You deserve a pat on the back for the hard work you are completing in this section. Rewards help you to pay attention to you triumphs, not your setbacks. Rewards will create good feelings and propel you to want to work harder to reach your goals. Whenever you have completed or achieved one of your goals, treat yourself to one of the items on your list.

You can also reward yourself by giving yourself positive affirmations when achieving a goal. Cut them out and post in visible spots everywhere! If these don't work for your goal, write your own on sticky notes!

I had fruits and veggies for my snacks today!	I smiled every time I looked in the mirror.	I exercised today!
I love ME!	I'm feeling good about myself.	I am a work in progress, and that's OK with me.
I am getting there!	I enjoyed my exercise today!	I had a healthy lunch.

When you have a positive self-image, you value and respect your body; you are also more likely to feel good about living a healthy lifestyle.

— Chad Tackett

PHYSICAL WELL-BEING

BODY IMAGE

Step 7: Tips for Motivated Behavior Modification

A HEALTHY FOOD PLAN
- Select food from all of the food groups to maintain a healthy balance with your daily food plan.
- Be aware of binge eating or eating even when you are not hungry, eating too fast, eating when you feel anxious, lonely or depressed, and eating beyond your normal comfort level.
- Become more aware of the portions that you eat at a meal. Avoid buffet eating, unless the food is healthy.
- Avoid diet pills, quick loss fixes, and fad food plans. Many of these fads rely on methods that often don't work, offer strategies that ensure weight loss, but not permanent weight loss.

EXERCISE
- Physical activity is an integral part of weight management. Because many people have a sedentary work or lifestyle, it can be difficult for them to allow time for adequate physical activity. Try to avoid many of the modern labor-saving devices such as escalators, elevators and driving when you can walk.
- Be consistent when you begin exercising. Many people begin an exercise regimen and are motivated at the beginning, but their enthusiasm wanes. Set realistic goals and adjust your body weight slowly over time. A gradual lifestyle change is best.
- Join an exercise gym to feel supported in your efforts to be healthy and adjust your weight.

SELF-ESTEEM
- Don't become obsessed with your body weight. Accept yourself as a worthwhile person regardless of how much you weigh. If you want to gain or lose weight, it is important that your efforts be for health reasons as well as appearance.
- Don't blame yourself for past failures in weight management. Learn lessons from these attempts so that you can be successful now as you set new and realistic goals.
- Don't compare yourself to other people, especially people in the media. They often have trainers and chefs who ensure that they remain and look fit, as well as photographs that have had computer adjustments. You may not have these luxuries.
- Become aware of the negative self-talk that relates to your body image. That little voice inside your head can lead to unmotivated behavior. Become aware of these voices and shut them out. Say "Stop!" Substitute positive self-talk. Meditate for a few seconds until the voice goes away, or wear a rubber band and snap it on your wrist when you begin to listen to this internal self-defeating chatter.

Information about Unhealthy Body Images

Many people are searching for the elusive perfect body, which can never be attained. Rather than achieving physical wellness, these people often harm themselves even more. Some people are so obsessed with their body image, that they ultimately develop serious health problems:

1. **Anorexia Nervosa** is an eating disorder in which people have a distorted body image and think they are fat even though they are very thin, sometimes emaciated. Anorexics become obsessed and have an unusual relationship with food, grocery shopping, and eating habits.
2. **Bulimia Nervosa** is also an eating disorder in which healthy-looking people experience recurring episodes of binge eating and purging to maintain their weight.
3. **Muscle Dysmorphia** is common among body-builders who, regardless of their muscle mass, continue to weight train in search of the "perfect" body.

If you feel that you are experiencing symptoms of any of these unhealthy body image behaviors, consult a physician immediately.

SECTION V

NUTRITION

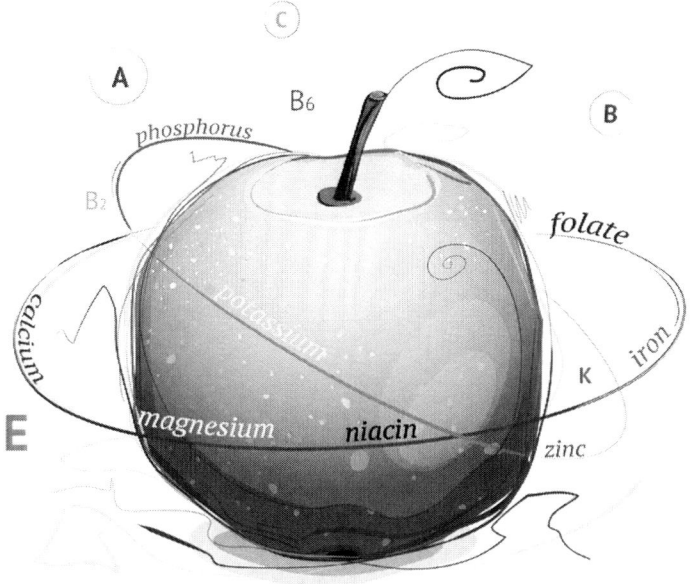

Those who think they have no time for healthy eating, will sooner or later have to find time for illness.

— **Edward Stanley**

Name _____

Date _____

PHYSICAL WELL-BEING

PHYSICAL WELL-BEING

NUTRITION

Step 1: Self-Assessment Introduction and Directions

Nutrition is the study of nutrients in the food you eat and how your body processes those nutrients. Proper nutrition is critical to developing and maintaining a sense of physical wellness. Nutrition covers the spectrum of eating behaviors including dietary guidelines for good health, reading food labels and the development a personal nutritional program.

The Nutrition Self-Assessment is designed to help you explore your nutritional choices. It contains two parts: Nutritional Planning Habits and Nutritional Eating Habits.

This self-assessment contains 26 statements related to the daily nutritional choices you make. Read each statement and decide the extent to which the statement describes you.

3 = Always   2 = Sometimes   1 = Rarely

My nutritional choices . . .

I start the day with a good breakfast. 3   (2)   1

In the above statement, the circled 2 means that the person completing the self-assessment sometimes begins the day with a good breakfast.

This is not a test and there are no right or wrong answers. Do not spend too much time thinking about your answers. Your initial response will be the most true for you. Be sure to respond to every statement.

Turn the page and complete the Self-Assessment

PHYSICAL WELL-BEING

NUTRITION

Step 1: Self-Assessment

3 = Always   2 = Sometimes   1 = Rarely

My nutritional choices . . .

I start the day with a good breakfast	3	2	1
I eat small portions at several intervals throughout the day	3	2	1
I make good low-fat lunch choices	3	2	1
I eat a healthy dinner	3	2	1
I avoid snacking too much after dinner	3	2	1
I bake, broil, or roast rather than fry foods	3	2	1
I keep my food safe to eat by proper handling and temperature control	3	2	1
I eat healthy snacks	3	2	1
I plan my meals and shop ahead	3	2	1
I eat healthy foods at home as often as possible	3	2	1
When shopping, I read nutrition labels before buying	3	2	1
I cook foods to the proper temperature	3	2	1
I avoid using too much salt	3	2	1
I try not to eat too many high cholesterol foods each day	3	2	1
I drink a minimum of six glasses of water daily (48 ounces)	3	2	1
I limit my daily intake of alcohol	3	2	1
I limit my intake of caffeine (soda, tea, coffee, chocolate)	3	2	1
I consume the appropriate amount of protein daily	3	2	1
I limit my intake of fatty meats	3	2	1
I consume a sufficient amount of vegetables daily	3	2	1
I consume a sufficient amount of fruits daily	3	2	1
I limit the amount of sugar I eat daily	3	2	1
I consume servings from the major food groups daily	3	2	1
I eat a variety of grains daily	3	2	1
I do not eat junk food or processed food	3	2	1
I shop for foods that are low in fat, sugar and caffeine, and moderate in calories	3	2	1

TOTAL _____

Go to the Scoring Directions on the next page

PHYSICAL WELL-BEING

NUTRITION

Step 1: Self-Assessment Scoring Directions

The Nutrition Self-Assessment provides you with information about the effectiveness of your nutritional planning and eating choices. Add the numbers you have circled and put that total on the line marked TOTAL at the end of the page.

Now, transfer your total to this line below:

Nutrition Total _____

Profile Interpretation

Total Score	Result	Indications
26 – 43	Low	If you scored in this range, a few of your nutritional choices are healthy, but you will need to develop many more healthy nutrition habits.
44 – 60	Moderate	If you scored in this range, some of your nutritional choices are healthy. Continue to develop more healthy nutrition habits.
61 – 78	High	If you scored in this range, most of your nutritional choices are healthy. Continue to develop healthy nutritional habits.

By responding to this self-assessment, you have identified the types of choices you make in nutritional planning and eating. Following are descriptions of the self-assessment. Complete the exercises that follow to help you learn more about how your nutritional choices affect your physical wellness, and help you make motivated behavioral modifications in your life. No matter how you scored, low, moderate or high, you will benefit by completing these exercises.

PHYSICAL WELL-BEING

NUTRITION

Step 1: Self-Assessment Descriptions

Nutritional Planning and Eating Habits – People scoring high on this self-assessment follow the dietary guidelines for good health. They are aware of healthy choices and use it as a practical guide for effectively evaluating their nutritional intake. When shopping they read the nutritional facts that contain information on food labels about nutrients of major concern to them. They are aware of the hazards of eating too much junk and processed food, and carefully plan the meals they cook at home.

People scoring high on this self-assessment are cognizant of the nutritional values of food they eat, and they make every attempt to avoid foods that are not healthy for them. They are aware of how much alcohol they consume and limit it to a reasonable amount. They understand the negative effects that too many fats and carbohydrates, and too much sugar and sodium can have on the body. They eat well-balanced meals that include foods from all of the major food groups. They eat a healthy amount of fresh fruits and vegetables and choose healthy snacks.

Step 2: Recognize and Develop a Support System

To make the behavioral changes you desire, you need to recognize your current support system and identify who might be helpful to you. Not every supportive person in your life will be helpful for each of your challenges. Complete the following table with people who might be in your healthy nutrition support system.

Supporter	How This Person Can Support Me	How I Can Contact This Person
My wife	By eating the same types of healthy foods that I do.	At home or on the phone when wanting to talk about tonight's dinner.

Keep this list handy. Call, email or text when you need support.

PHYSICAL WELL-BEING

NUTRITION

Step 3: Keep a Journal

The following journaling questions are designed to help you think conscientiously about the nutritional planning and eating behaviors you want to change. Remember, your thinking can affect how motivated you are to make healthy changes in your behavior.

How can you improve your overall nutritional plan?

How can you better plan meals so that you can eat healthier?

What types of healthy snacks can you eat?

How can you begin eating more healthy foods? What foods are they?

What small or big changes with your eating habits are you prepared to make, starting now?

PHYSICAL WELL-BEING

NUTRITION

Step 4: Set Goals

A well-conceived action plan will help you to achieve your nutritional goals by keeping you motivated. For your action plan, identify both the behavior you want to change and specific goals, or smaller goals required to reach your ultimate nutritional goals.

The behavior I want to change is _____

Goals need to be SMART:

Specific, Measureable, Attainable, Realistic and Time-Specific

Goals	How I Will Measure Each Goal	How is Each Goal Attainable and Realistic?	Time Deadline	How This Change Will Help Me
Stop eating less junk food.	I eat junk food almost every day. I need to reduce it to once a week.	I will only go to fast food restaurants that serve healthy meals.	One month from now.	I will have less stomach problems.

If you are having trouble identifying goals, consult the TIPS, page ____.

PHYSICAL WELL-BEING

NUTRITION

Step 5: Monitor My Behavior – Nutritional Habits

Monitoring your progress toward your goals will help to reinforce your behavior. Keeping track of your behaviors through logs will help you determine what you have accomplished at given times. Periodic re-evaluations are vital for your success. Once you reach your goal(s), set new ones to improve or maintain what you have already achieved. Use a separate page for each change.

EXAMPLE:

My healthy behavior change Decide ahead of time what to eat rather than right before I eat.

My goal Plan my meals and buy foods a week ahead of time.

Date	My Accomplishment	How It Felt
1/1/2014	I planned a week's menus and shopped today.	It was a lot do but I felt relief because it will be easier all week.

- -

Nutritional Habits

My healthy behavior change _____

My goal _____

Date	My Accomplishment	How It Felt

(Continued on the next page)

PHYSICAL WELL-BEING

NUTRITION

Step 5: Monitor My Behavior
Nutritional Habits *(Continued)*

How do you anticipate that new nutritional habits can make a difference for you?

_____
_____
_____

What obstacles do you anticipate in instituting healthy planning and eating habits in your life?

_____
_____
_____

What motivates you to change your nutritional habits?

_____
_____
_____

How do your present nutritional habits affect your overall wellness now?

_____
_____
_____

How can your present nutritional habits affect your overall wellness in the future?

_____
_____
_____

What questions about nutrition do you have?

_____
_____
_____

PHYSICAL WELL-BEING

NUTRITION

Step 6: Reward Myself

People who reward themselves are more likely to continue to improve their nutritional planning than people who don't! The challenge is to decide what reward would motivate you to reach a goal you have set. Your reward needs to be something that will give you the incentive to achieve your goals. It needs to be within your budget and something you'll be excited about. If you are buying yourself something, be sure your reward is something you wouldn't ordinarily buy or do.

Brainstorm possible rewards.
- Rewards that would be meaningful to me _____
- Small rewards I provide for myself _____
- Large rewards I provide for myself _____
- Things that would not cost money and would be fun _____
- Rewards that I can afford and that would be fun _____
- Rewards that I can enjoy alone _____
- Rewards I can enjoy with people who support me _____

You deserve a pat on the back for the hard work you are completing in this section. Rewards help you to pay attention to you triumphs, not your setbacks. Rewards will create good feelings and propel you to want to work harder to reach your goals. Whenever you have completed or achieved one of your goals, treat yourself to one of the items on your list.

You can also reward yourself by giving yourself positive affirmations when achieving a goal. Cut them out and post in visible spots everywhere! If these don't work for your goal, write your own on sticky notes!

I shopped today for the whole week.	I enjoy drinking more water.	I feel accomplished when I eat healthy.
No junk food today!	I am doing well.	**I love eating more fruit.**
I feel better!	**I have discovered healthy snacks!**	*It feels good to eat healthy.*

According to the World Health Organization,
A healthy diet can protect the human body against certain types of diseases, in particular non-communicable diseases such as obesity, diabetes, cardiovascular diseases, some types of cancer and skeletal conditions. . . . Healthy eating is a good opportunity to enrich life by experimenting with different foods from different cultures, origins and with different ways to prepare food.

PHYSICAL WELL-BEING

NUTRITION

Step 7: Tips for Motivated Behavior Modification

Nutritional Planning Habits

- When shopping for food, remember to read the labels before buying. Look for the amount of fat, carbohydrates, protein, sugar, sodium, and cholesterol the item contains.

- Rely on the social support network you developed in Step 2. These are people who can motivate you when you get tired of eating healthy and want to revert to your old eating habits. Remember to return the favor when they need your support.

- Always wash hands and preparation surfaces before handling food and after handling food.

- Keep refrigerator clean.

- Store food in their wrappers.

- Wash food thoroughly.

- Use paper towels to dry foods.

- Discard towels after each use.

- Refrigerate any products you do not eat.

- Pack a lunch to avoid being tempted to eat junk and/or processed foods.

- Only go to fast food restaurants that include healthy menu choices.

- Plan the meals you will prepare at home. Take time to develop a meal plan that consists of healthy ingredients to avoid becoming frustrated when you don't have food in the house and then are tempted to eat unhealthy food or rely on junk foods.

Nutritional Eating Habits

- Avoid adding too much salt (sodium) or sugar to your foods.

- Avoid eating foods that add too much fat, saturated fat, and/or cholesterol in your diet.

- Drink plenty of water each day to maintain good health.

- Eat low-fat food as an evening snack. Try popcorn, yogurt, fresh fruits or vegetables.

- Plan to eat a balanced diet containing appropriate servings from each food group.

- If you drink alcoholic beverages, do so in moderation.

- Excellent and complete food information can be found on www.nutritiondata.com.

SECTION VI
ADDICTION

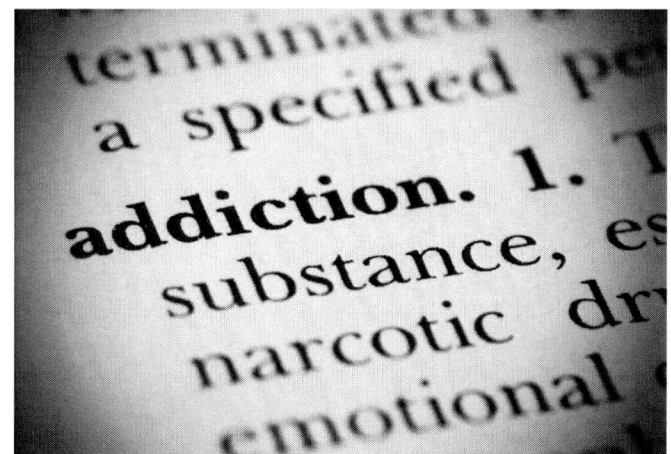

You know you are addicted to Facebook when you log off Facebook, turn your computer off, go to bed, roll over and log onto your Facebook from your phone one last time for the night.

— **Azgraybebly Josland**

Name _____

Date _____

PHYSICAL WELL-BEING

ADDICTION

Step 1: Self-Assessment Introduction and Directions

An addiction is a reliance on something or someone. An innocent habit may become an addiction which has physical, mental, social and emotional consequences. An addiction goes beyond what a person is addicted to or how the person participates in a habit. An addiction becomes extremely difficult to quit due to psychological, emotional, habitual and physical withdrawal symptoms. People with an addictive personality have a tendency to become addicted easily to substances, activities, thoughts or behaviors. The *Addiction Self-Assessment* can help you identify and explore your likelihood of becoming addicted to any substances, activities, thoughts or behaviors.

The self-assessment contains 20 statements. With YES or NO as your choice, read each of the statements and circle which best describes whether the statement applies to you or not.

My Possible Addiction *Playing Golf*

I am excessively addicted to this behavior/activity . . . . YES   (NO)

In the above statement, the circled NO means that the statement is not like the test taker.

This is not a test and there are no right or wrong answers. Do not spend too much time thinking about your answers. Your initial response will be the most true for you. Be sure to respond to every statement.

Check your possible addictions:

Substances	Activities	Thoughts and Behaviors
❑ Alcohol	❑ Body building	❑ Arson
❑ Caffeine	❑ Card games	❑ Betting
❑ Chocolate	❑ Collecting items obsessively	❑ Bullying, sadism, masochism
❑ Cocaine	❑ Email	❑ Crime
❑ Diuretics	❑ Exercising too much	❑ Cyber sex
❑ Illegal drugs	❑ Gambling	❑ Eating disorders
❑ Legal drugs	❑ Internet	❑ Fanaticizing excessively
❑ Marijuana	❑ Online games	❑ Love obsessively
❑ Medications	❑ Sex	❑ Money
❑ Nicotine	❑ Shopping	❑ Over-sleeping
❑ Over the counter medications	❑ Shopping online	❑ Pornography
❑ Prescription drugs	❑ Sports obsession	❑ Procrastination
❑ Solvents	❑ Texting	❑ Relationship neediness
❑ Steroids	❑ Thrill-seeking behaviors	❑ Risky behavior
❑ Sugar	❑ Video games	❑ Self-injury
❑ Tranquilizers	❑ Working	❑ Stealing

Turn the page and complete the Self-Assessment

PHYSICAL WELL-BEING

ADDICTION

Step 1: Self-Assessment

(Complete a separate self-assessment page for each of your addictions noted on page 89)

My Possible Addiction _____

I am excessively addicted to this behavior/activity	YES	NO
When under stress, I often resort to this behavior	YES	NO
I get a craving for this substance or activity	YES	NO
I have a hard time stopping the behavior once I begin	YES	NO
I tend to be compulsively about this behavior	YES	NO
I deny I am involved with this if someone asks	YES	NO
I feel like this is taking over my life	YES	NO
When I want this, I want it immediately	YES	NO
I get a high feeling from this behavior/substance	YES	NO
I have been involved with this substance/behavior for over a year	YES	NO
I get withdrawal symptoms if I am not engaged with this substance/behavior	YES	NO
I cannot stop doing this once I have started	YES	NO
I lie to others about my involvement with this behavior	YES	NO
I have tried to stop this, but I cannot	YES	NO
I gravitate to people who also engage in this behavior	YES	NO
My health suffers because I am involved with this behavior/substance so often	YES	NO
I become anxious if I cannot readily engage in this behavior or with this substance	YES	NO
I often engage in this behavior without even thinking	YES	NO
I get preoccupied and constantly think about this behavior	YES	NO
I constantly increase the amount of time I engage in this behavior	YES	NO

Total number of YES answers = _____

(Go to the Scoring Directions on the next page)

PHYSICAL WELL-BEING

ADDICTION

Step 1: Self-Assessment Scoring Directions

An addiction often begins as sampling a pleasurable substance, joining an activity, or a thought or behavior in which you voluntarily participate, but which ends in compulsion, a loss of control of your actions, and the need to repeat the action even though it may be harmful to you. An addiction actually becomes part of your personality.

COMMON ADDICTIONS

- Substances
- Activities
- Thoughts & Behaviors

For the self-assessment you just completed, add the number of Yes answers that you circled. Transfer the total to the space below.

Addiction Total = _____

Addiction Self-Assessment Profile Interpretation

1. **If you find yourself having the types of thought and behaviors listed in the assessment, you are showing signs of an addiction. You can overcome addictions to substances, activities and thoughts and behaviors if you are motivated to do so. The following exercises will be helpful to you.**

2. **If you checked at least one activity in any of the three categories (substances, activities, thoughts & behaviors), it is very important for you to complete the following exercises.**

The following steps are designed to help you identify and overcome your addictions to substances, activities, thoughts and behaviors. Continue completing the remaining steps.

© 2014 WHOLE PERSON ASSOCIATES, 210 WEST MICHIGAN ST., DULUTH MN 55802-1908 ▪ 800-247-6789

PHYSICAL WELL-BEING

ADDICTION

Step 2: Recognize and Develop a Support System

To make the behavioral changes you desire, you need to recognize your current support system and identify who might be helpful to you. Not every supportive person in your life will be helpful for each of your challenges. Complete the following table with people who might be able to support you with your addictive behavior.

Supporter	How This Person Can Support Me	How I Can Contact This Person
My therapist	By giving me someone I trust to talk to when I need help.	Phone: 1-000-000-0000.

Keep this list handy. Call, email or text when you need support.

PHYSICAL WELL-BEING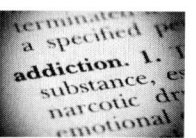

ADDICTION

Step 3: Keep a Journal

The following journaling questions are designed to help you think seriously about the behaviors you want to change. Remember, your thinking can affect how motivated you are to make healthy changes in your behavior. *(Complete a separate self-assessment page for each of your addictions noted on page 89.)*

My possible addiction _____

When did you begin engaging in your addiction?
_____
_____
_____

What prompted you to start?
_____
_____
_____

How do you cope with it?
_____
_____
_____

How do you have trouble coping with it?
_____
_____
_____

How do you benefit from it?
_____
_____
_____

How do you not benefit from it?
_____
_____
_____

PHYSICAL WELL-BEING

ADDICTION

Step 4: Set Goals

A well-conceived action plan will help you to achieve your addiction-reduction goals by keeping you motivated. For your action plan, identify both the behavior you want to change and specific goals, or smaller goals required to reach your ultimate goals for addiction reduction.

The behavior I want to change is _____

Goals need to be SMART:
Specific, Measureable, Attainable, Realistic and Time-Specific

Goals	How I Will Measure Each Goal	How is Each Goal Attainable and Realistic?	Time Deadline	How This Change Will Help Me
To play less golf.	I currently play 6-7 days per week, I want to eventually reduce it to 2 times per week.	I will find other hobbies to do as well.	My birthday.	I will have more time for my wife, my grandchildren and myself.

If you are having trouble identifying goals, consult the TIPS, page 102.

PHYSICAL WELL-BEING

ADDICTION

Step 5: Monitor My Behavior – Substances

Monitoring your progress toward your goals will help to reinforce your behavior. Keeping track of your behaviors through logs will help you determine what you have accomplished at given times. Periodic re-evaluations are vital for your success. Once you reach your goal(s), set new ones to improve or maintain what you have already achieved. Use a separate page for each change.

EXAMPLE:
My healthy behavior change *I should stop drinking so much coffee.*

My goal *Have one cup of coffee at breakfast and no more during the rest of the day.*

Date	My Accomplishment	How It Felt
1/1/2014	I had only 3 cups of coffee all day.	I had a headache, but I did it.

- -

Substances

My healthy behavior change _____

My goal _____

Date	My Accomplishment	How It Felt

(Continued on the next page)

PHYSICAL WELL-BEING

ADDICTION

Step 5: Monitor My Behavior
Substances (Continued)

Who encourages you to continue with your addiction to substances? How does this pressure affect you?
___
___
___

Who encourages you to stop your addiction? How does this pressure affect you?
___
___
___

What do you gain from your addiction?
___
___
___

What do you lose from your addiction?
___
___
___

What obstacles do you anticipate in stopping your addiction.
___
___
___

What can you do to stop your addiction?
___
___
___

PHYSICAL WELL-BEING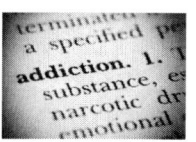

ADDICTION

Step 5: Monitor My Behavior – Activities

Monitoring your progress toward your goals will help to reinforce your behavior. Keeping track of your behaviors through logs will help you determine what you have accomplished at given times. Periodic re-evaluations are vital for your success. Once you reach your goal(s), set new ones to improve or maintain what you have already achieved. Use a separate page for each change.

EXAMPLE:

My healthy behavior change *Try to stop my gambling.*

My goal *Stop by the time we go on vacation in 6 months.*

Date	My Accomplishment	How It Felt
1/1/2014	I went to a therapist.	Disappointed. The therapist and I did not connect. I will try another.

Activities

My healthy behavior change _____

My goal _____

Date	My Accomplishment	How It Felt

(Continued on the next page)

PHYSICAL WELL-BEING

ADDICTION

Step 5: Monitoring My Behavior
Activities *(Continued)*

Who encourages you to continue with your addiction to these activities? How does this pressure affect you?

_____
_____
_____

Who encourages you to stop your addiction? How does this pressure affect you?

_____
_____
_____

What do you gain from your addiction?

_____
_____
_____

What do you lose from your addiction?

_____
_____
_____

What obstacles do you anticipate in stopping your addiction.

_____
_____
_____

What can you do to stop your addiction?

_____
_____
_____

PHYSICAL WELL-BEING

ADDICTION

Step 5: Monitor My Behavior – Thoughts and Behaviors

Monitoring your progress toward your goals will help to reinforce your behavior. Keeping track of your behaviors through logs will help you determine what you have accomplished at given times. Periodic re-evaluations are vital for your success. Once you reach your goal(s), set new ones to improve or maintain what you have already achieved. Use a separate page for each change.

EXAMPLE:

My healthy behavior change *I procrastinate and everything takes forever to get done.*

My goal *Stop procrastinating by setting dates and times for task completion.*

Date	My Accomplishment	How It Felt
1/1/2014	I finished most of what I needed to on time.	I felt encouraged because I received praise.

✂ -

Thoughts and Behaviors

My healthy behavior change _____

My goal _____

Date	My Accomplishment	How It Felt

(Continued on the next page)

PHYSICAL WELL-BEING

ADDICTION

Step 5: Monitoring My Behavior
Thoughts and Behaviors *(Continued)*

What is so enticing about the thoughts and behaviors to which you are addicted?

_____
_____
_____

When and how did these addictions begin?

_____
_____
_____

Who is your payoff for these addictions?

_____
_____
_____

What is the downside of this addiction?

_____
_____
_____

What do you lose from these thoughts and behaviors?

_____
_____
_____

How would your life be without this addiction?

_____
_____
_____

PHYSICAL WELL-BEING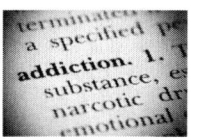

ADDICTION

Step 6: Reward Myself

People who reward themselves are more likely to continue to improve their addiction than people who don't! The challenge is to decide what reward would motivate you to reach a goal you have set. Your reward needs to be something that will give you the incentive to achieve your goals. It needs to be within your budget and something you'll be excited about. If you are buying yourself something, be sure your reward is something you wouldn't ordinarily buy or do.

Brainstorm possible rewards.
- Rewards that would be meaningful to me _____
- Small rewards I provide for myself _____
- Large rewards I provide for myself _____
- Things that would not cost money and would be fun _____
- Rewards that I can afford and that would be fun _____
- Rewards that I can enjoy alone _____
- Rewards I can enjoy with people who support me _____

You deserve a pat on the back for the hard work you are completing in this section. Rewards help you to pay attention to you triumphs, not your setbacks. Rewards will create good feelings and propel you to want to work harder to reach your goals. Whenever you have completed or achieved one of your goals, treat yourself to one of the items on your list.

You can also reward yourself by giving yourself positive affirmations when achieving a goal. Cut them out and post in visible spots everywhere! If these don't work for your goal, write your own on sticky notes!

I CAN DO IT!	I said "NO" today.	I want to be OK!
I listened to a CD and felt calmer.	I am proud of myself for trying.	**I am grouchy, but I know it will get better.**
I am saving money!	**I feel better after exercising!**	*I want a better life.*

We are addicted to our thoughts.
We cannot change anything if we cannot change our thinking.

— **Santosh Kalwar**

PHYSICAL WELL-BEING

ADDICTION

Step 7: Tips for Motivated Behavior Modification

Common characteristics of an addiction:

1. Obsession with the activity, substance, or thought/behavior and cannot stop thinking about it.
2. Compulsive attention to the addiction which usually causes harm (problems in school, with friends and family, and with people in the community).
3. Engage in the activity over and over even though one wants to stop.
4. Withdrawing from the addiction causes withdrawal symptoms whether it is a psychological addiction (shopping) or a physical addiction (opiate).
5. Loss of control of when, how often, and how much time spent with the activity.
6. Denial of having an addiction.

Tips:

- Taper off participating in your substance, activity, thought or behavior. Consult a physician if you are at risk for physical withdrawal from a substance (*alcohol, pain killers, tranquilizers, etc.*).

- Be assertive with friends and family who pressure you to continue your addiction. Rely on your support system for help. Describe your situation (*When you want me to smoke…*), your feelings (*I feel afraid that you will leave me if I refuse*), what you want (*I don't care if you smoke but I don't want to*), and the result (*If you continue to pressure me to smoke, I will leave you*).

- Make a list of all of the financial costs related to your addiction. Put that money in a container and use it for something special.

- Search for healthy alternatives to the addiction.

- Develop interests in your life other than your addiction. Remember that balance in your life is important. If you are a workaholic working eighty hours per week, you will not have time for relaxation or time with family and friends.

- Think about all of the ways you have changed negatively since engaging in your addiction(s).

- Remember, you have control over your addiction and yourself. Your addiction does not have control over you. Take control.

- Talk with someone else who has overcome an addiction. How did the person do it?

- Concentrate on all of the benefits of recovery. How will you be better off without your addiction(s)?

- Find a replacement for your addiction. Therefore, when you feel anxious or stressed and find yourself about to indulge in your addiction, have a healthy replacement for it.

- Become aware of how negative thinking keeps your addiction alive. For example, that little voice inside your head may be saying such things as "One more won't hurt" or "Everyone's doing it."

- Don't give in to peer pressure. Even adults often succumb to pressure from family and friends to continue engaging in an addiction that can be harmful.

- Notice that you may be engaging in an addictive substance, activity, thought or behavior as an escape from your problems. If so, consult a mental health professional.

SECTION VII
SAFETY

*At the end of the day,
the goals are simple:
safety and security.*

— **Jodi Rell**

Name _____

Date _____

PHYSICAL WELL-BEING

PHYSICAL WELL-BEING

SAFETY

Step 1: Self-Assessment Introduction and Directions

In our times, many people are worried about the threat of rising crime in the community, workplace, school, your vehicle and home. It is important to recognize and understand your level of personal safety.

This self-assessment will help you identify how well you are ensuring your safety. Circle the number that describes you.

In the following example, the circled NO indicate how much the statement is not descriptive of the person completing the inventory.

When it comes to personal safety at home . . .

I keep my doors locked at all times . . . . YES (NO)

This is not a test. Since there are no right or wrong answers, do not spend too much time thinking about your answers. Be sure to respond to every statement.

Turn the page and complete the Self-Assessment

PHYSICAL WELL-BEING

SAFETY

Step 1: Self-Assessment

When it comes to personal safety at home ...

I keep my doors locked at all times	YES	NO
I have smoke detectors that are in good working order	YES	NO
I have adequate home insurance	YES	NO
I have at least one fire extinguisher in the house	YES	NO
I have NO firearms or I keep them unloaded, hidden and locked up	YES	NO
I have an escape plan in case of an emergency	YES	NO
I maintain all heating and electrical sources	YES	NO

TOTAL 1 = _____

When it comes to personal safety while driving ...

I never go faster than the posted speed limit	YES	NO
I always buckle my seat belt	YES	NO
I never use alcohol or other drugs	YES	NO
I follow other drivers with at least 2-3 seconds distance	YES	NO
I do not accept phone calls or texts	YES	NO
I do not call or text other people	YES	NO
I am non-aggressive in traffic	YES	NO

TOTAL 2 = _____

When it comes to personal safety in my community ...

I avoid dark places	YES	NO
I remain aware of my surroundings	YES	NO
I stay away from isolated areas	YES	NO
I leave an uncomfortable situation	YES	NO
I don't keep a spare key outside my house	YES	NO
I use lights on timers when I'm not home	YES	NO
I get cash out of the ATM during the day	YES	NO

TOTAL 3 = _____

Go to the Scoring Directions on the next page

PHYSICAL WELL-BEING

SAFETY

Step 1: Self-Assessment Scoring Directions

The Safety Self-Assessment is designed to measure your personal safety habits at home, in your vehicle, and in your community. For each of the sections on the self-assessment you completed, count the YES responses you circled for each of the three sections. Place that total on the line marked TOTAL at the end of each section.

Then, transfer your totals to the spaces below:

TOTAL 1 = _____ Home

TOTAL 2 = _____ Driving a Vehicle

TOTAL 3 = _____ Community

Add these three scores (you will get a number from 0 to 21) to get your grand total for personal safety and place that number below:

GRAND TOTAL = _____

Self-Assessment Profile Interpretation

1. **If you said "No" to any of the items listed in the self-assessment, you are not living a safe life and you are jeopardizing your physical well-being. Be aware of the various ways that you are putting your own safety and the safety of others at risk. The following exercises will be helpful to you.**

2. **Next, look back over the activities listed for each of the three categories (Safety at Home, Safety While Driving a Vehicle, and Safety in Your Community) and identify activities that you said NO to. Think about ways that you can begin to live more safely.**

Self-Assessment Descriptions

Home – People scoring high (17–21) on this self-assessment tend to have good personal safety habits at home. They make sure their house is safe, have up-to-date electrical and heating components, and safe fire and carbon monoxide alarms. They keep their doors locked and have a safety plan for emergencies.

Driving a Vehicle – People scoring high (17–21) on this self-assessment tend to have good vehicle safety habits while driving. They do not drive aggressively, they use seatbelts and concentrate on traffic around them. They stay within the posted speed limits and do not use drugs, alcohol or phones when driving.

Community – People scoring high (17–21) on this self-assessment tend to be aware of the dangers in their community. They avoid dark, secluded places and know when situations get dangerous. They use their intuition and good judgment with the people in their community.

The following activities are designed to help you develop effective personal safety habits at home, in your vehicle, and in your community.

PHYSICAL WELL-BEING

ADDICTION

Step 2: Recognize and Develop a Support System

To make the behavioral changes you desire, you need to recognize your current support system and identify who might be helpful to you. Not every supportive person in your life will be helpful for each of your challenges. Complete the following table with people who might be able to support you with your safety behavior.

Supporter	How This Person Can Support Me	How I Can Contact This Person
My friend who is an occupational therapist	She can go through my house and see what is safe and what is not.	Phone or text: 135-7913 email: Sue@xyz.com

Keep this list handy. Call, email or text when you need support.

PHYSICAL WELL-BEING

SAFETY

Step 3: Keep a Journal

The following journaling questions are designed to help you think carefully about the behaviors with your safety. Remember, your thinking can affect how motivated you are to make healthy changes in your behavior.

What are some of the choices you have made in the past to protect your personal safety?

_____
_____
_____

What types of things do you do that you know are not safe, but do them anyway?

_____
_____
_____

What type of decision-making process do you use when making personal safety choices?

_____
_____
_____

What precautions do you take to remain safe?

_____
_____
_____

In what situations do you not feel safe?

_____
_____
_____

What can you do about it?

_____
_____
_____

PHYSICAL WELL-BEING

SAFETY

Step 4: Set Goals

A well-conceived action plan will help you to achieve your addiction-reduction goals by keeping you motivated. For your action plan, identify both the behavior you want to change and specific goals, or smaller goals required to reach your ultimate goals for addiction reduction.

The behavior I want to change is _____

Goals need to be SMART:

Specific, Measureable, Attainable, Realistic and Time-Specific

Goals	How I Will Measure Each Goal	How is Each Goal Attainable and Realistic?	Time Deadline	How This Change Will Help Me
Stop texting while driving.	Whether I do it or not.	I can think ahead and text before getting in the car.	Immediately.	I will not be in a car accident nor will I hurt someone else or myself.

If you are having trouble identifying goals, consult the TIPS, page 118.

PHYSICAL WELL-BEING

SAFETY

Step 5: Monitor My Behavior – Home

Monitoring your progress toward your goals will help to reinforce your behavior. Keeping track of your behaviors through logs will help you determine what you have accomplished at given times. Periodic re-evaluations are vital for your success. Once you reach your goal(s), set new ones to improve or maintain what you have already achieved. Use a separate page for each change.

EXAMPLE:

My healthy behavior change _We need smoke alarms._

My goal _Put smoke alarms in the house within the next week._

Date	My Accomplishment	How It Felt
1/1/2014	I called the local fire department today for info.	Wonderful. They gave me all the info I needed.

✂ -

Home

My healthy behavior change _____

My goal _____

Date	My Accomplishment	How It Felt

(Continued on the next page)

PHYSICAL WELL-BEING

SAFETY

Step 5: Monitor My Behavior
Home (Continued)

What potential hazards exist in your home?

_____
_____
_____
_____

Which rooms inside or items outdoors need the most attention?

_____
_____
_____
_____

How will you minimize the risks associated with personal safety in the home?

_____
_____
_____
_____

Who can help you make your home safe?

_____
_____
_____
_____

What can help you make your home safe, inside and out?

_____
_____
_____
_____

PHYSICAL WELL-BEING

SAFETY

Step 5: Monitor My Behavior – Driving

Monitoring your progress toward your goals will help to reinforce your behavior. Keeping track of your behaviors through logs will help you determine what you have accomplished at given times. Periodic re-evaluations are vital for your success. Once you reach your goal(s), set new ones to improve or maintain what you have already achieved. Use a separate page for each change.

EXAMPLE:
My healthy behavior change _Watch my speed._

My goal _NEVER go faster than the speed limit._

Date	My Accomplishment	How It Felt
1/1/2014	I drove today and never sped.	Slow, but good. I can't afford more tickets.

Driving

My healthy behavior change _____

My goal _____

Date	My Accomplishment	How It Felt

(Continued on the next page)

PHYSICAL WELL-BEING

ADDICTION

Step 5: Monitoring My Behavior
Driving (Continued)

What are some of the safe habits you have developed when driving a vehicle?

_____
_____
_____
_____

What are some of the unsafe habits you have developed when driving a vehicle?

_____
_____
_____
_____

How have your unsafe habits harmed you, or how could they have harmed you?

_____
_____
_____
_____

How have your unsafe habits harmed, or how could they have harmed one of your passengers or someone else?

_____
_____
_____
_____

Using three emotion words, how would you have felt if you harmed one of your passengers or someone else?

_____

PHYSICAL WELL-BEING

ADDICTION

Step 5: Monitor My Behavior – Community

Monitoring your progress toward your goals will help to reinforce your behavior. Keeping track of your behaviors through logs will help you determine what you have accomplished at given times. Periodic re-evaluations are vital for your success. Once you reach your goal(s), set new ones to improve or maintain what you have already achieved. Use a separate page for each change.

EXAMPLE:

My healthy behavior change Recruit neighbors to help finance the repair of ruts in the street.

My goal To make the street safer.

Date	My Accomplishment	How It Felt
1/1/2014	I went to three neighbors today and they all said they'd help.	It warmed my heart.

✂ -

Community

My healthy behavior change _____

My goal _____

Date	My Accomplishment	How It Felt

(Continued on the next page)

PHYSICAL WELL-BEING

SAFETY

Step 5: Monitoring My Behavior
Community (Continued)

Who in your community is living in unsafe conditions? How can you help this family or person?

___

What safety hazards are inherent in your community?

___

What can you do about them?

___

Have you ever had a complaint about your community?

___

Have you ever attended a town meeting? Called a council person? Gone to a council meeting? Why or why not?

___

PHYSICAL WELL-BEING

SAFETY

Step 6: Reward Myself

People who reward themselves are more likely to continue to keep safe than people who don't! The challenge is to decide what reward would motivate you to reach a safety goal.

Your reward needs to be something that will give you the incentive to achieve your goals. It needs to be within your budget and something you'll be excited about. If you are buying yourself something, be sure your reward is something you wouldn't ordinarily buy or do.

Brainstorm possible rewards.
- Rewards that would be meaningful to me _____
- Small rewards I provide for myself _____
- Large rewards I provide for myself _____
- Things that would not cost money and would be fun _____
- Rewards that I can afford and that would be fun _____
- Rewards that I can enjoy alone _____
- Rewards I can enjoy with people who support me _____

You deserve a pat on the back for the hard work you are completing in this section. Rewards help you to pay attention to you triumphs, not your setbacks. Rewards will create good feelings and propel you to want to work harder to reach your goals. Whenever you have completed or achieved one of your goals, treat yourself to one of the items on your list.

You can also reward yourself by giving yourself positive affirmations when achieving a goal. Cut them out and post in visible spots everywhere! If these don't work for your goal, write your own on sticky notes!

I helped a neighbor today!	I'm driving better!	I feel good about myself when I get involved in helping my community.
I learned how to fix my front steps.	I called the police when I saw someone being abused.	**I haven't had a ticket for a long time.**
I keep my front sidewalk swept for people who are walkers.	**I now check the air in my tires regularly.**	I removed throw rugs where my mom could trip.

Texting while driving increases the risk of accident 23.2 times over unimpaired driving.

— **Virginia Tech Transportation Institute**

PHYSICAL WELL-BEING

SAFETY

Step 7: Tips for Motivated Behavior Modification

Home Safety

- Keep outside doors locked at all times.
- Have chain locks put on your doors and do not open doors to people you don't know well.
- Have a peep-hole or a way to check before opening the door.
- Plan an escape route in case of an emergency (fire, carbon monoxide leak, etc.).
- Install smoke and carbon monoxide detectors and make sure that they are in good working order.
- If you keep firearms in your home, make sure that they are unloaded, locked up and hidden away.

Vehicle Safety

- Safe driving needs to be your priority when driving any type of vehicle or cycle.
- Stay within the posted speed limit when driving.
- Don't let other drivers or passengers pressure you to go faster.
- Do not follow other drivers too closely in case the driver needs to stop quickly.
- Never text or speak on the telephone while driving.
- Do nothing to incite another driver, even if you are upset with their driving.
- If you are on a long trip, take breaks often.
- If driving with another driver, switch from time to time.
- Always wear a properly fitted helmet when riding a bicycle, motorcycle, motorized scooter, ATV or off-road vehicle. Helmets have been shown to be effective in preventing traumatic brain injuries.

Community Safety

- Avoid dark places and do not walk alone in unfamiliar areas.
- Always be aware of your surroundings and remove yourself from the situation if you feel uncomfortable.
- Ensure that your cell phone is always fully charged.
- Carry your cell phone at all times.
- Avoid individuals who have a history of aggressive behavior, limited social skills, or demonstrate a violent attitude.
- Vary your routine and walking patterns to be less predictable.

Whole Person Associates is the leading publisher of training resources for professionals who empower people to create and maintain healthy lifestyles. Our creative resources will help you work effectively with your clients in the areas of stress management, wellness promotion, mental health and life skills.

Please visit us at our web site: **www.wholeperson.com**. You can check out our entire line of products, place an order, request our print catalog, and sign up for our monthly special notifications.

Whole Person Associates

800-247-6789

PHYSICAL WELL-BEING